NATURE DETECTION AND CONSERVATION

This is a book about nature – and
conservation. It is a book about what can
be done, and why and how. It also tells
you what *you* yourself can do in your own
environment — even if you live in a town;
and where and how to study and explore
nature.

JEAN MELLANBY

NATURE DETECTION AND CONSERVATION

Illustrated by Vera Croxford

Consultant Editor: Anne Wood

CAROUSEL BOOKS
A DIVISION OF TRANSWORLD PUBLISHERS LTD

NATURE DETECTION AND CONSERVATION

A CAROUSEL BOOK 0 552 54019 6

First publication in Great Britain

PRINTING HISTORY
Carousel edition published 1972
Carousel edition reprinted 1974

Carousel Books are published by
Transworld Publishers Ltd.,
Cavendish House, 57–59 Uxbridge Road,
Ealing, London, W.5

Made and printed in Great Britain by
Cox & Wyman Ltd., London, Reading and Fakenham

CONTENTS

5

NOTES

PERSONAL CHOICE

THE wild life of Britain is extraordinarily interesting. Perhaps it is not as dramatic as that of the jungle and tropical forest, but on a smaller scale it is equally fascinating. Unfortunately today it may be seriously threatened. The countryside is being swallowed up, as land is required for houses, schools, factories, motorways, airports, reservoirs, and everything else needed by a growing population with rising standards of life. It is feared that pollution will cause birds to be poisoned, butterflies to disappear, and fish to die in their thousands in polluted water. Changes in agricultural practice, such as more intensive farming and the removal of hedges, may also be damaging to wild life.

On the other hand, there is a more widespread concern for the future of nature in Britain, and more is being done about it. Many major decisions affecting our environment will have to be taken on a nation-wide, or even a world-wide, scale, but all of us can play some part in the work. What may seem a trivial action when taken by one person can have tremendous effects when followed by all of us. Conservation is too often thought of as a passive attitude, one of leaving things alone, but it is really an activity, to be pursued in the ordinary circumstances of our daily lives, in town or country.

A hundred years ago a good naturalist was a good collector. He robbed birds' nests, and caught butterflies, or dug up rare wild orchids. The results can be seen in museums all over the country, in dusty cabinets and drawers full of specimens. The foundations of important scientific work were laid, but if people today continued to collect on the same scale great damage could be done. Even then, some kinds of birds disappeared. One beautiful butterfly, the large copper, was exterminated in East Anglia partly by over-collecting. Fortunately our way of

LARGE COPPER BUTTERFLY L. DISPAR BATAVA

thinking has changed. Today, rather than collecting dead specimens, naturalists are more interested in *ecology*, the study of living things in their own surroundings and the relationships between different parts of the natural world. Bird behaviour is much more interesting than egg collecting. One observer decided to watch a wren visiting her nest. He watched all day, and found that between sunrise and sunset she came to the nest to feed her young or for other reasons 1217 times, in a working day of 15 hours and 45 minutes. Another watched a moorhen pulling a piece of plastic sheeting over herself as she sat on her nest in the rain. Botanists were puzzled by lines of weeds in fields, until they realized the seeds were being dropped by birds perched on telegraph wires. On one day in the year, hundreds of people all over Britain get up in the middle of the night, to listen to bird song, and they record the exact time each bird joins in the dawn chorus, plotting which kinds of birds get up first. Another nation-wide scheme is the recording of butterflies, birds, flowers, and other forms of wild life, wherever they occur. The results are analysed by computer at the Monks Wood research laboratories in Huntingdonshire, run by the Nature Conservancy, so that eventually it can be worked out how many of each species really exist in our country and where they are. You can join in this recording if you are a reasonably careful observer and can fill up the details on a form. Alternatively, a real feeling of achievement comes from photographing wild life, because it demands patience, skill, ingenuity, and imagination. The tape recording of bird song and animal noises is another absorbing interest. If you prefer to collect, the variety of nature is well illustrated by collections of leaf prints, leaf skeletons, or bark rubbings, to give just one example of a kind of collecting that is not harmful.

LEAF PRINTS, SKELETON LEAVES, AND BARK RUBBINGS

1. TO MAKE BLACK AND WHITE PRINTS OF LEAVES, hold a tin lid or plate over a lighted candle until it is blackened. Add a few drops of olive oil or machine oil, and mix well. Rub the mixture over the back or underside of the leaf, with your finger. Then press the leaf on to a sheet of white paper, black side down, cover it with newspaper and rub gently.

2. TO MAKE COLOURED PRINTS OF LEAVES, use powder paints (mixed very thickly), or shoe polish, of the right colours. Apply it to the back of the leaves, instead of the black mixture suggested in (1), and then print as before.

3. TO MAKE SKELETON LEAVES, use rather old, tough leaves, not fresh green foliage. Soak them in cabbage water, or simmer them gently for about an hour in boiling water with a tablespoon of washing soda in it. Then carefully brush away the tissue of the leaves, and soak the skeletons overnight in a solution of water and domestic bleach, before rinsing and drying them between sheets of blotting paper.

4. TO MAKE BARK RUBBINGS OF TREES, hold a sheet of thin white paper against the bark of a tree, and rub the surface from side to side, *or* up and down, using heel ball or cobbler's wax. Another way is to use an ordinary white candle, and then paint over your rubbing with Indian ink.

HOW TO MAKE BLACK AND WHITE PRINTS OF LEAVES (i)

1

2

3

Blotting
paper

4

5 print

LEAF SKELETONS

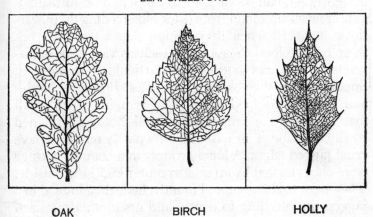

OAK   BIRCH   HOLLY

Even today, though, if a very rare bird is known to be nesting, such as the osprey, a 24 hour a day watch has to be kept, to prevent the nest being robbed. Many wild flowers are becoming scarce, because too many are picked, before they have time to seed and spread themselves. A famous naturalist has suggested butterfly nets may have to be banned, because it is too easy for people to catch too many butterflies in them. Even frogs are becoming scarce, partly because too many are collected for classroom study and examination purposes. We all have to watch ourselves to make sure our private interests and hobbies do not become harmful. There are far too many of us in the world today for us all to be able to do exactly what we want and go exactly where we wish to go. People can do great harm to the countryside simply by being there. Some special kinds of place – mountain areas, sand dunes, some woodlands – are damaged by being trampled. There are still far too many forest and heath fires, caused by carelessness. They bring great suffering to birds and beasts as well as causing economic damage. Litter is still a problem. It is not just unsightly – it can be very hurtful to wild life. Birds may garner unsuitable food from litter bins, feeding their nestlings on bread when they cannot digest anything but their proper food. Scavengers such as rats may be attracted. Tins and bottles are particularly dangerous. Small animals such as mice and voles climb into bottles and may be trapped there. The remains of 28 small mammals were once found in a milk bottle abandoned by the roadside. Tins with lids only partly removed have cruel jagged edges. A lonely couple in a country cottage were once startled by an odd irregular knocking outside. They went to the door and found a hedgehog lodged in a jagged tin, bleeding to death, and unable to drag itself clear. Traffic on roads causes great slaughter. The Automobile Association in America reported in 1968 that at least a million creatures *a day* were killed by cars on American roads. In Britain also many birds are killed, as well as deer, rabbits, moles, hares and badgers. So are hedgehogs, in great numbers, though there is some evidence now that they are at least learning to remove themselves quickly instead of 'freezing' when frightened. Detailed information is lacking about the extent of this loss on roads. Groups of people in different areas could keep regular and exact records of how many dead creatures they found in measured lengths of road over a

HOW TO PREPARE BONES AND SKULLS

Here are some simple ways of preparing bones and skulls of birds and animals, if you wish to preserve these for study. Use only animals you find dead or killed on the roads, or others such as rabbits and hares which you can buy at the butcher's.

1. A small animal, such as a shrew or a mouse, can be buried in an ant hill. The ants will eat all the surplus flesh in a few weeks.

2. Larger animals, such as rabbits, can be buried in earth, and then left for at least a year.

3. Any animal carcase or part of it can be boiled until the flesh can be picked off with tweezers or a darning needle. The boiling is best done on a camp fire in the garden, using old tins or billy cans. Wash the bones after boiling them, and put them in a household bleach to whiten them.

4. After partial boiling, a small skull, such as that of a bird, can be hung by a thread in an aquarium containing a lot of tadpoles, which will eat the flesh.

period. Often the bodies are not very damaged, so that skeletons, especially skulls, could be collected for study.

HUNTING AND SHOOTING

This last kind of killing is a pity, but it is not usually deliberate. What then about hunting? Many people who love wild life and the countryside cannot bear to think of foxes and deer being hunted to death. They find it impossible to condone any form of blood sports or killing simply for pleasure. Others feel that though the chase itself may be cruel, sportsmen do no harm to conservation, because they know how important it is to protect a breeding stock of any game animal or bird and they do not kill too many for replacement. Sportsmen also see the need for maintaining living space and the right conditions for wild life, if for no other reason than to protect their sport. But many of them genuinely care for the countryside. The Duke of Edinburgh has written: *'I am always amazed that so many townspeople seem to be incapable of understanding that hunting and conservation are now entirely compatible. ... They simply will not, or do not wish to recognize that in most parts of the world the leadership in conservation has come from experienced hunting sportsmen.'* And there are sometimes strong arguments for 'culling' – the reduction of a population of animals, for instance deer, or seals, when their numbers have grown too great in certain areas for their own health or proper survival. But these matters are very debatable, and even conservationists do not always agree with each other. Whatever the case for fox or deer hunting, none of them would approve of otter-hunting, still organized in parts of Britain, although otters are becoming scarce and do very little damage. There are more than a dozen packs of otterhounds listed in the sporting journals. (There are more than two hundred packs of foxhounds.) As for badger digging and baiting, still said to be among village sports and pastimes, it always was sheer brutality, and should most certainly be stopped.

Talk of hunting takes us far beyond Britain. Throughout the world beautiful animals are being exterminated because their furs have a high market value. Fashion bears a heavy responsibility for the hunting of these wild creatures. Ocelots and jaguars are slaughtered in South America; cheetahs in Africa; leopards in Asia. All the large cats are in danger of extinction, although they are among the world's rarest and most beautiful animals. Would you wear a leopard skin coat, if you knew that fourteen of these animals had been killed to make that coat? And this is only the beginning. Whales are slaughtered and are in danger of extermination because whale oil is used in cosmetics and other preparations. Turtles are becoming rare partly because people eat turtle soup. Crocodiles and alligators are killed to make handbags and shoes. Expensive scent is based on musk from civet cats.

Great damage to the animal world is also inflicted by wasteful and cruel methods of hunting animals for Zoos, wild life parks, circuses, and the pet trade, although the first two of these have done great service in protecting rare species. The whole subject of animals in captivity raises questions to which we may give different answers. Naturalists and nature lovers are individuals. They do not all think alike. One would enjoy seeing elephants performing in the circus ring; another would be sickened by the sight of animals trained to do tricks. One would keep wild animals as pets; another would consider it wrong to take such creatures from their natural surroundings, and tame them, making them into something different from what they are by nature.

17

Nature conservation is not about whether we should love animals as pets. Nor does it mean that all animals, in all circumstances, everywhere, should be protected or left alone. Things do not stand still, especially as there has already been almost world-wide interference in the processes of nature by man for his own ends. Intelligent management is now required, in the interests of the natural world.

Conservation *does* imply the protection of *species* of wild life, if not of all individual animals, and too many species have already been lost or are on the brink of extinction. Fortunately we are now much more alive to this danger than we used to be, and thanks to such organizations as the World Wildlife Fund, there is a continuous policy of watchfulness all over the world, to try to make sure we do not lose any further species. Allied to the protection of species is the protection of the places where they live (their habitats), because many kinds of animals, birds, plants, and other forms of life, have very specific needs that must be met if they are to survive and reproduce. How this can best be done, to perpetuate a rich variety of life, is a matter for urgent thought and action.

For these reasons, this is a book about conservation in Britain – its various forms, what can be done, and why, and how; what you yourself can do, in your own environment, even if you live in a town, and your opportunities of going to the countryside are limited; and where and how to study the living pattern of nature, so that you can learn what may need to be done in the future. Nature conservation requires a sympathetic understanding of the living pattern, of which man himself is a part, and it implies a respect for life as such. We have to become more aware of what is going on around us. Nowadays, in the twentieth century, man often seems to be living in an artificial world of his own making, too far removed from the rest of the natural world. Perhaps he needs to learn afresh that he cannot survive if he destroys too much of nature's network – the fabric of life in a living world. And while learning that lesson, he should protect other forms of life as much as he can, trying not to leave the world a poorer and a duller place for his children and grandchildren.

NATURE'S NETWORK

SCAVENGERS AND DECOMPOSERS

APART from the ones killed on the roads, it is really quite rare in nature to find the dead bodies of animals and birds, considering how many millions of them die every year. What happens to them? A naturalist decided to find out by watching. The body of a dead fallow deer was found in Epping Forest. It had been killed by poachers who took part of it for venison and abandoned the rest. It was left on the ground for observation. Within two days badgers started to eat the softer parts of the flesh, having broken open the stomach. Carrion crows, magpies, and a fox were seen near. Flies and maggots soon appeared; insects sheltering and feeding attracted other birds, such as a spotted flycatcher and a blackbird; and within six weeks the bones had been picked clean.

Animal droppings also disappear quite quickly, some less speedily than others. Horse droppings are attacked by flies, maggots and beetles. There is even a fungus which grows only on such droppings and helps to decompose them. A cowpat disappears in a rather different way, often eaten and decomposed from below so that a dried-up skin may be left on top. Dead fish and any other dead bodies in water are soon used as larders by a host of hungry scavengers. So are dead trees and plants. You can test this process of decomposition for yourself. If you find a dead sparrow and can leave it on grass or earth (preferably where cats can't get at it and spoil your experiment) you can record which species can be found eating there, and in what order they come, and how long it takes for the body to disappear. If you don't like using a dead body, try something like half an orange. Doing this several times a year you would find great differences in the rate of disappearance; warm damp weather is the most favourable – guess why! An old orchard with windfall apples lying in it is very attractive to many forms of life. Even horses have been known to get drunk on fermented apples!

Many of nature's scavengers can easily be seen – the bluebottles, earthworms, and burying beetles, for instance. Others are very small – mites, springtails, eelworms, among them. Others again are microscopic. In one gram of soil there are literally millions of micro-organisms, such as bacteria, fungi, algae and others, their work being to feed on and break down the remains of dead animals and plants. They are sometimes called nature's dustmen, or refuse collectors. If you think this whole subject rather disgusting, think how much more unpleasant the world would be if remains were not dealt with in this way. It has been suggested that one day the whole island of New Zealand will sink under a load of accumulated ordure, because mammals have been introduced there comparatively recently and the resulting absence of dung beetles and decomposing bacteria has led to piles of dung. And this explains, too, why some forms of litter are so much worse than others. An apple core thrown down at a picnic, or a banana skin, will fairly soon be got rid of, but nature's dustmen cannot deal with tin cans, glass bottles, or plastic bags. They will eventually tackle paper, but not tinfoil.

The scavengers and decomposers are very useful in keeping the world tidy, but their work is really much more important than that. They form an essential link in the cycle of life, by which materials essential for life and growth are sent circulating round and round, instead of just being used and then discarded.

In the old Yorkshire song, 'On Ilkley Moor 'baht 'aht', a young man is told to wear a hat when he goes courting Mary Jane on the moor. If he doesn't, he will catch cold, and die; then the worms will eat him up; then ducks will eat the worms; then people will eat the ducks, and then, the man is told, 'We shall 'ave etten thee!' This illustrates that nothing is lost in nature, becoming instead food for some other organism. But the song is not quite accurate in describing the cycle of life. It misses out the *green* element.

Green is a marvellous colour. If you look out of the window on a railway journey and watch the fields and woods flashing by, you can see hundreds of different shades of green, varying from blue black in the shadows to golden in the sunlight. If you try to paint out of doors you need to mix many different tints. But in plants green is also a marvellous *working* colour. The green colouring matter in leaves (*chlorophyll*) has the wonderful ability to absorb the light energy of the sun, and use it to start the process of *photosynthesis* (literally 'building up by means of light') by which carbon dioxide and water are combined to produce basic food substances. The carbon dioxide is taken in from the air into the leaves, and water, containing such chemicals as nitrogen, sulphur, calcium, magnesium, phosphorous, and iron, is absorbed by the roots. With energy derived from respiration, and the consumption of atmospheric oxygen, the plant produces the carbohydrates, proteins, and fats needed for body tissue. So green plants produce food from non-food. No wonder they have been called food factories; they are really rather elaborate chemical works. Without the light of the sun, and without green plants, our living world could not exist. Scientists today are thinking in terms of by-passing one or other or both of these two requirements for making food, but so far the idea of feeding the world in these new ways belongs to science fiction rather than to reality.

You can test for yourself the importance of sunlight for growing plants. Any plants kept in the dark or in artificial light soon die. Bulbs such as daffodils will begin to grow, because their first sources of food are stored inside them, but as soon as they begin to shoot they have to be brought into the light. If you leave them in the dark you will eventually find a nasty twisted mass of white shoots, just as you would if you left a bag of old potatoes in the dark in spring, when they are beginning to put out shoots from their eyes. To test the ability of plants to convert chemicals into tissue, you can put a plant in a jam jar of water, so that the plant itself rests on the rim and the roots are in water, and then see if you can keep the plant alive by adding drops of a general chemical fertilizer from a gardening shop. This may or may not work; it depends on whether the fertilizer is right for the plant, and whether you get the quantities right.

After the green plants, or *primary producers*, have made their food, they can build up their tissues and are then available as food for other organisms. Much of the food they produce, however, cannot be eaten by any hungry creature that comes along. Man can eat lettuce, or cabbage; but he can't digest grass. Nebuchadnezzar, in the Bible, is said to have eaten grass, but it must have made him very sick, as it would a pet dog or cat. The *primary consumers*, or *herbivores*, are the grazing

23

animals such as cattle and sheep. In turn these primary consumers are themselves eaten by flesh-eaters, the *secondary consumers*, that is animals such as lions, or wolves, or birds like owls or hawks. In their turn these creatures may become food for other flesh-eating animals which would then be called *tertiary consumers*. If you had a plate of cold meat and salad for your lunch, you would be a primary consumer when you ate the lettuce, and a secondary consumer if you were eating cold lamb. If you were eating cold pork, from a pig which might itself have been fed on meat scraps, you would also be a tertiary consumer.

And finally in the chain we come back to our dustmen – the scavengers and decomposers in nature, including the organisms that feed on decayed plants (being thus primary consumers) and the others that feed on the remains of animals (thus being secondary or tertiary consumers). When micro-organisms finally break down all the remains, they are returning to the soil, or to water, the mineral salts needed again by plants, thus completing the circle. They are ensuring that the essential substances required for growth will always be there for green plants to use.

Today the term *biogeochemical cycle* is used to describe this process. *Bio* is life; *geo* is earth or soil; *chemical* here means the substances needed by plants to make living tissue, by means of light energy, and *cycle* means a series of happenings that keeps repeating itself like the turning of a bicycle wheel. So the biogeochemical cycle is the process by which non-living or inorganic substances move from the non-living world through the living world and back again, in a continuous repeat performance.

When you walk through a meadow, or visit a wood, or look at a pond, you can see at once that each has different kinds of plants and animals living in it. In nature very little is accidental, or random. Always, although often modified by human interference, there are basic patterns of life, and the study of them is what ecology is all about. In an oak wood, for instance, besides the oak trees themselves, you are likely to find ash trees, and sycamores, and many smaller trees such as hazels, and maples; there will be primroses, bluebells, wood anemones, and violets; in sunny patches between trees you may see silver-washed fritillary butterflies, among a host of other insects; you may hear robins, tits, finches, and woodpeckers; and almost certainly there will be squirrels there. On moorland, by contrast, there will be bracken, and ling heather, and mountain ash trees; instead of fritillaries, the emperor moth is more characteristic; cuckoos, red grouse, and skylarks will be seen, or heard; there will be no squirrels, but very possibly hares. A pond is different again. Sticklebacks, waterlilies, moorhens, and frogs may be there. So these places are often called *habitats*, meaning places where different forms of life find the conditions they need, and can live in association with each other. A cave, an igloo, or a house may be a human habitat. Your dog may be a habitat for fleas or worms!

Ecology, however, is a comparatively new science, and the terms used in it are still being developed or expanded in meaning. Some of the places described as habitats, such as a wood or a pond, might now be described as *ecosystems* rather than habitats. The difference might be that an ecosystem has some power of self-renewal. The different parts of which it is composed operate in such a way as to keep it in being as a system.

25

Indeed, an ecosystem has four parts – the inorganic substances needed by plants, the primary producers or plants themselves, the consumers, and the decomposers; and through these parts a continuous circulation of food takes place by means of the biogeochemical cycle. A wood is an ecosystem, because it may be able to maintain itself by regeneration, producing enough seedling trees to keep itself going as a wood with all the other plants and animals it shelters. A cowpat is a habitat, because although communities of animals and plants may find a home there, they do not produce another cowpat!

LIFE IN AN OAK TREE

1. AN OAK TREE NEEDS SUNLIGHT, SOIL AND WATER. IT CAN DRINK 100 GALLONS OF WATER A DAY; IT CAN GROW 125 FEET HIGH, 40 FEET IN GIRTH, SINK ITS ROOTS 15 FEET DEEP AND WEIGH 100 TONS. IT PROVIDES HOMES FOR 500 SPECIES OF INSECTS AND NESTS FOR 20 SPECIES OF BIRDS. ITS ACORNS PROVIDE FOOD FOR MANY ANIMALS AND BIRDS.

2. TAWNY OWL ROOSTS AND NESTS IN THE HOLE IN THE OAK. IT ALSO PREYS ON BIRDS AND INSECTS THAT LIVE THERE.

3. GREAT TIT NESTS IN A HOLE IN THE OAK AND FEEDS ON INSECTS THAT LIVE THERE.

4. GREY SQUIRREL MAKES ITS BREEDING NEST AND WINTER NEST IN THE OAK. IT ALSO EATS ACORNS AND BURIES THEM FOR FUTURE USE. SOME ACORNS WILL GERMINATE AND GROW INTO SAPLINGS.

5. STAG BEETLE LIVES IN DECAYED WOOD AND FALLEN BRANCHES.

6. EARTHWORMS ENRICH THE SOIL BY DIGESTING FALLEN LEAVES.

7. BADGER SLEEPS IN HIS UNDERGROUND SET ON A BED OF OAK LEAVES. HE INCLUDES IN HIS VARIED DIET ACORNS AND NESTLINGS THAT HAVE FALLEN OUT OF THEIR NESTS IN THE TREES. HE MIGHT USE THE OAK AS A SCRATCHING POST TO SHARPEN HIS CLAWS.

Briefly, then, an ecosystem is a *community of plants and animals adapted to living in the ecosystem as a special environment, and maintained more or less as a self-contained unit by means of the continuous interchange of life-giving substances.* In this sense, the world is itself an ecosystem, when you are thinking of life as a whole, but used in this way the word ceases to be useful. Some writers group all the major habitats of the world into ecosystems, recognizing only four types – that is, aquatic, terrestrial, soil, and artificial or man-made. Others would divide up the world rather differently, into *biomes*, meaning major areas of the world with their own climatic conditions and special communities of life – some of these being grassland, tropical forest, coniferous forest, and desert regions. Then the term ecosystem would refer to smaller environments, such as hedgerows, meadows, ponds, or woods, where the two elements are present – (*a*) that the environment in question is a unit supporting groups or associations of plants and animals needing that environment, and (*b*) that the different parts of the ecosystem can work together so as to maintain it as a system. In practice no ecosystem is completely self-perpetuating, and none is really self-contained or isolated as a unit. The one factor of bird migration means that there is considerable coming and going between different systems.

If you are a 'muddy boot' ecologist, that is, one who likes to go out and see things for himself, the best way to learn about ecosystems is to go out and look for one. Perhaps the most accessible and at the same time most fascinating is a perfectly ordinary pond. Of course ponds come in all sorts of shapes and sizes. It's quite interesting just to dig a hole in the garden and keep it full of water, to see what happens – it will become an ecosystem in time! Best of all is an old, natural, undisturbed, never dried-up, rather shallow pond, with squelchy wet edges, where perhaps a cow sometimes stands, drinking and swishing her tail. Having found such a pond, you may see quite a lot by just sitting in the sunshine and watching. Making and using a bird hide in which you can sit and watch unseen will widen the possibilities. Or you can try to make a survey of the pond and the life it sustains. There are all sorts of different ways of tackling a project like this. One way is to get a length of rope and lay it down on the ground, one end on the bank, leading inwards to the pond. It will then lie across the bank, the marshy area, and then the swamp, and part of the shallow water. Then you can list every plant the rope touches, and every animal, big or small, you can see on either side of the rope. This will indicate the zonation, or the way life is organized in areas at different depths of water or different degrees of wetness at the edge.

Considering the pond as an ecosystem, you will find the four parts present that actually define it as an ecosystem. First and foremost, in the water of the pond and in the soil round it, and the sediment at the bottom, there will be the oxygen all plants need (the amount of it will greatly affect the life of the pond) and the mineral salts such as the phosphates, ammonium salts, and other nutrients, often enough to form a very rich and soupy brew which will help to form a very productive system. Much of this material is ready for use by the plants that need it, and it is continually being added to by the decomposers of plant and animal remains. Secondly, there are the plants growing round and in the pond, some in soil at the edge, some floating on top of the water but with their roots at the bottom, like water lilies, some floating aquatic plants with their roots dangling in the water, and some submerged aquatics, such as the Canadian pondweed. Thirdly, there is the animal life of freshwater, including the herbivores such as tadpoles

29

and caddis larvae, and the carnivores such as frogs and toads, fish like perch and pike, most water beetles, water spiders, and dragonfly nymphs. And lastly there are the scavengers, such as freshwater shrimps and water worms, and the decomposers such as the bacteria and fungi feeding on dead plants and animals and helping to release chemical substances to be re-used.

Another approach to the study of ponds as ecosystems is to consider the degree of pollution to be found there. One cause of pollution is too much organic matter getting into the water. Suppose a cesspool from a house leaked into the pool, or drainage from a farmyard somehow reached it – or even suppose a very heavy leaf fall in autumn filled up a pond. If there is this excess of organic matter, the bacteria decomposing it may use up too much oxygen – more than is replaced by seeping through the surface of the water and that given off by submerged plants. Then the bacteria produce marsh gas (methane) and substances with a bad smell, such as ammonia and hydrogen sulphide. This can be tested by experiment as well as by the nose. If you can get a bit of turmeric paper from a chemistry set try dipping it in the water. It will turn brown if ammonia is present. To test for hydrogen sulphide, which smells like bad eggs, use lead acetate paper, because sulphides turn it black. Try holding a piece over a pan of boiling cabbage, or over a newly-opened bad egg. To test the water, half fill a glass tube with it, then wedge the paper in with the cork, so that the paper is held above the water. If it darkens, the water is giving off the gas.

Another way of measuring pollution in water is to look for indicator animals. For streams and rivers (not stagnant water in ponds) they have been classed in this way:

stonefly nymph mayfly nymph	A	If these animals are present, the water is clean.
caddis fly larva freshwater shrimp	B	These can tolerate more pollution than A.
water louse 'bloodworm' (chironomid larva	C	Finds of these animals only (and D) indicate pollution fairly serious.
sludge worm and only those breathing air, e.g. rat-tailed maggot	D	Finds of these only indicate highly polluted water.

This gives a scale of pollution for running water, once you have learnt to identify the animals. You will need a magnifying glass to do so, but you can soon put together a do-it-yourself kit for this kind of water pollution and make notes of the results in different streams. It is more difficult to work out indicator animals for ponds, but if you found *no* animals there, or only those classed as D in the table, you could certainly conclude the pond was highly polluted.

FOOD CHAINS AND FOOD WEBS

Within an ecosystem, there is a whole complex of feeding relationships. The simplest form of such a relationship is a chain, with two, three or four links in it. As an example, rabbits eat grass, and foxes eat rabbits. So this sequence makes a food chain and is written:

                    grass→rabbits→foxes
Other simple food chains are:
        blackberries→flies→spiders→birds→cats
        phytoplankton (tiny plants in the sea)→
            zooplankton (tiny animals in the sea)→
                copepods (rather bigger sea animals)→
                        herring→
                            cod→
                                man

   In practice, feeding relationships are seldom as simple
as this. Each link in the chain interconnects with other
chains. Take for instance the simple chain grass→rabbit
→fox. What else eats grass besides rabbits? and what do
they eat? and what eats them? what else eats rabbits,
besides foxes? and what eats them? what else do foxes
eat? Suppose they eat chickens. What do chickens eat,
and what eats them? If you think these relationships are
simple, try working out some for yourself. (To find out
what animals eat, you can analyse their droppings, or
if you find the bodies of dead animals while they are
still *fresh*, you can slit their stomachs and examine the
contents.) In fact, isolated food chains do not occur
in nature, and the pattern of feeding relationships
within an ecosystem is better described as a *food
web*.
   Whether chain or web, the pattern is of tremendous
importance for conservation, because if a poison gets
into the pattern at any time, it may be passed on to
different parts of it, with quite unforeseen results. Some
years ago in Britain farmers dressed their seed corn with
dieldrin, to prevent it from being attacked by wheat
bulb fly larvae in the fields. Pigeons began to eat the seed
– it was said they even learnt to dig it up from the
ground and eat it in large quantities. As pigeons are a
great agricultural pest, perhaps no one would have

worried very much about this, but the pigeons were eaten by other animals. Predatory birds such as hawks, which fed on poisoned pigeons, were also killed, and their numbers in Britain fell alarmingly. There were cases of particularly intelligent badgers lurking beneath pigeon roosts, having learnt that some would fall down dead; but as the ones that fell first were those affected by the poison, the badgers were also killed.

Stable poisons like dieldrin and other organo-chlorines have had other effects. Dieldrin used in sheep dips may have poisoned golden eagles in Scotland, not always killing them, but affecting their fertility and breeding success, because the eagles fed on dead sheep carcases lying on the hills. And suppose a farmer casually threw an empty tin of sheep dip into a ditch or pond, not thinking any harm, that poison in water could do immense damage, poisoning fish, and then the birds that fed on the fish. Some organisms, particularly fish, seem to have the ability of concentrating poison in their tissues, so that although not killed, they retain some of the poison without excreting it, so that it remains ready to poison the next link in the chain. A heron eating many affected fish with small quantities in the tissues would then die.

Examination of poisoned birds or fish is a very technical matter requiring skill and equipment. But accidental poisoning of water can sometimes be indicated by experiment. If you can get some Universal Indicator paper (perhaps from a chemistry set), cut a piece into strips, and dip them in various liquids. Vinegar, which is an acid, turns it red; ammonia, an alkali, turns it blue. When you dip the paper into pure water, it will not change colour much. In water with too much acid in it, the paper will turn pinkish, brownish, and red, at the extreme. In water with too much of any alkali, the paper will turn green, and then blue. Gardening shops often sell small kits for testing soil or water, and they are very convenient because they include a colour chart.

SUCCESSION AND CONSERVATION

When an unforeseen element begins to affect one part of an ecosystem, many other parts will also be affected. The new factor may be a poison, such as dieldrin in seed dressings, but is sometimes quite 'natural'. In the autumn of 1953, the disease of myxomatosis appeared in Britain, probably as the result of a mosquito infected with the virus being blown across the Channel from France, where the disease had been introduced, and starting the outbreak in Kent. Rabbits began to die in their thousands, and the rabbit population of the country was reduced by at least ninety per cent. The ecological effects – on other animals, and especially on vegetation – were immense; we still do not quite know what the total effect has been. Again, sometimes foreign elements are introduced into an ecosystem, with significant results. When farms were started in East Anglia to breed coypu for their fur, some of these animals escaped, and began to breed in the dykes and on river banks. Large scale programmes of trapping and killing had to be initiated to prevent widespread damage. Introduced animals (and even plants) can become 'aggressive', flourishing at the expense of native flora and fauna, and sometimes becoming a real menace. Sometimes, too, within an ecosystem, one type of organism may become too successful. In some way the controls over its numbers cease to operate; the population increases rapidly; the animal is said to 'swarm' and the process is finally brought to an abrupt end by some kind of disaster (the suicidal rush of lemmings to the sea may possibly be one of the effects of swarming).

Even without these dramas in nature, communities of

34

plants and animals are continuously changing, adapting to change in and outside their own communities, often very slowly, but noticeably, and according to recognizable stages, and this process of orderly change is called *ecological succession*. It is of tremendous importance for nature conservation and as it can be observed at many different stages it is worth considering one or two of them.

Primary succession is said to start with a piece of land that has not previously supported life at all. Suppose you have a plain rock surface, with nothing growing on it. Gradually it may be weathered, by rain, frost, and wind. In the small cracks and hollows made in this way on the surface water will collect and dissolve some of the minerals on the rock surface. Then simple plants may establish themselves; lichens may be first, blown in spore form. Eventually there may be pockets for windborne dust and soil, plus organic matter from dead lichens. This provides some sort of habitat for animals such as mites, ants, and spiders; their dead remains add to the soil; mosses may move in; soon there are fresh animal arrivals, such as mites and other groups. Moss holds down the soil; plants decay; more soil is formed. Birds and insects may visit the pockets of soil; soon grasses appear; more animals and nematodes; more soil; then small shrubs and trees finally germinate there. The order of species appearing depends on local conditions. Finally you may get fairly stable conditions described as climax vegetation.

A different type of succession, sometimes called *secondary succession*, may begin in an area where there has been some catastrophic or dramatic event. After a forest fire, for instance, life gets itself going again. You might be able to watch the process if you could find an area of heathland that had been ravaged by fire, and see how and in what order plants and trees re-establish

35

themselves, and how insects and animals move back into a devastated area. Again, everything depends on local conditions, but somehow, plants and animals will recolonize the most unpropitious places; nature is very tough. But the area will not be quite the same, at any rate for a very long time, if left alone.

You can watch quite another kind of succession in a habitat such as a tree. When it is flourishing, it gives food and shelter to a multitude of other organisms, from lichens and mosses on its trunk, to birds in its branches and perhaps badgers at its roots. As it grows old, and dies, the birds have to find new homes, and the insects that have lived there; an old stump may be colonized by quite a different group of birds, and may support fungi; finally the wood of the tree will decompose, and a host of bacteria and decomposers will return substances to the soil.

But why should this worry conservationists? It is a fascinating process to observe, over periods of time, but it may convert interesting and delightful areas into something much less attractive. One of the most delightful parts of the English natural scene is the meadows and pasture of grasslands on chalk. Wild flowers there may include cowslips, birdsfoot trefoil, the horseshoe vetch, the rock rose, and the wild thyme. Brilliant blue butterflies will be there; and skylarks also. Rarities such as different orchids may be found. So if a stretch of this type of area can be preserved, we may well rejoice. But, and this is a big but, left alone such an area may lose all its attractions. If it is not grazed by rabbits, or sheep, or cows, untidy and unattractive scrubby bushes and brambles will grow there, and trees such as willow, maples and elms; a thicket will develop. Other plants and birds will enter, and grass will disappear as sun and moisture are taken up by trees. The community will change, and all that was valued in the

36

meadow may disappear. So, such an area has to be managed, to retain its interest; and this is the sort of problem the practical conservationist has to consider.

MAN THE MENACE

If ecology has anything to teach, it is that nature is indivisible. Everything in nature is intricately meshed together. Many of us were brought up to believe that nature is 'red in tooth and claw', as if every part of nature were at war with every other part. It is true there may be intense competition, at different times and in different places, but generally the different parts of nature are interdependent. Plants and animals share the same conditions, they help each other, they cannot live without each other.

Into this complex and delicately-balanced pattern of life on earth, man has come blundering with little regard for anything but his own immediate needs. He has hunted animals to extinction, over-grazed large areas and turned them into dustbowls, hacked down forests, and dammed up rivers. Today science and technology have given him almost unlimited power. Vast schemes are being discussed. Should we melt polar icecaps – blast mountain ranges – drain seas – flood deserts? We are taking enormous risks. Our efforts to produce more and more food are having far-reaching effects on nature and vegetation. We may be poisoning land, sea, and air. We are certainly exhausting some of the world's resources, using up fossil fuels and some minerals at a disastrous rate. We are even allowing our own numbers to 'swarm', and soon there may be far more people on earth than can well be supported. It has even been suggested, among other forecasts of doom, that supersonic aircraft may disturb the upper atmosphere to such an extent that dangerous radiation from the sun might reach the earth, with unimaginable effects on life there.

In this situation, nature can act as an early warning system. If trees die because of a sulphur-laden atmosphere, or fish are found to be full of mercury because of wastes poured into the sea, this may be an indication that we are making mistakes. Dead birds, disappearing butterflies – these too may be signs that we have gone too far. Nature conservation is far from what some people imagine it to be – the mere protection of a few animals and flowers. It becomes a question of whether man can survive at all, in the world he is creating.

It has been said that if you wish to see a specimen of the most dangerous and destructive animal on earth, all you have to do is look into a mirror. But this is only one side of the question. If you wish to see a specimen of the most intelligent, the most successful, and the most

ALL WILD-LIFE IS AFFECTED BY POLLUTANTS. EVEN THE LONG-TAILED FIELD MOUSE AND SNOWDROPS MAY EVENTUALLY DISAPPEAR.

powerful animal in the world, again you can do so by looking into a mirror. Man has done great harm to the living world, but in many ways he has made the earth a more beautiful and interesting place. Once he sees the need for an intelligent policy of nature conservation, he will cease to be quite so dangerous to the world or to himself.

3

PESTS AND POLLUTION IN THE HOME

LIFE ON MAN

MAN'S body is a walking zoo. Just as he is dependent on plants and animals for his food and very existence, so there are other plants and animals which could not exist without him. Your own body can carry quite a rich variety of flora and fauna; there is plenty of life on man. Although you can't grow mushrooms on your skin, there are other fungi that can't grow anywhere else. Ringworm, on the scalp, and athlete's foot, are among the plant parasites that live on human beings. The insects that do the same include head lice, body lice, and fleas, and there is also the scabies mite which burrows under skin to lay its eggs. There are other occasional insect attackers, such as mosquitoes, which make blood-sucking visits. Bees and wasps may sting, and ants may bite. Then there are viruses and micro-organisms that cause colds and such diseases as pneumonia, polio, and dysentery. But not all the parasites on the human body are harmful. None of us could digest our food without the bacteria living in the gut. The internal digestive system is dependent on its flora.

Perhaps you could work out a diagram to illustrate how man's body is a habitat for other forms of life, and how his waste products and finally his bones and flesh are returned to earth and water to be re-cycled. Part of nature's network is dependent on him. But he is dependent on nature – and another part of the same diagram could show how he needs nature for his food – vegetable, animal, fish – and how he uses natural products for his home (wood for beams and floors, reeds for thatch), clothes (leather, wool, silk, cotton) and furniture (wood, wool, leather). Nature could function without man, but not man without nature.

THE LIVING HOUSE

A house too can be a perfect menagerie. Wherever possible, human habitations are invaded by flies, bluebottles, spiders, rats, mice, cockroaches, woodworm, deathwatch beetles, silver fish, bookworms, and other creatures. Older houses have sparrows and house martins in the eaves, and perhaps bats in the roof space. There is also life in the larder. Yeast is alive, and there may well be moulds on bread and fruit. Another plant in older houses in the hated dry rot, a very damaging fungus.

Housewives wage constant warfare on all these invaders. There is plenty of material here for the ardent naturalist, but it is not of a kind we can easily tolerate. But do we need to keep our houses as clean and sterile as hospital wards? Often when spring cleaning we find clusters of ladybirds on window-sills. They do no harm, and they are not in any way dirty. When warmer weather arrives they will disappear and do nothing but good in the garden. Butterflies, too, are often found behind pictures, or in odd corners behind cupboards and other furniture, as they like to hibernate in warm dry places. Too much dusting will disturb them. They should never be touched or moved. They will fly again when they are ready and will then leave by any open window. Spiders' webs are very interesting to watch –

again, they are not dirty. Must they always be swept away? Spiders may be quite useful catching flies.

Our homes make quite a large contribution to pollution. Coal burnt on ordinary domestic fires, in open grates, is much the most serious source of atmospheric pollution. If more of us were able to use smokeless fuel, or change to gas or electricity for heating, the problem of smog would be greatly reduced. And housewives use detergents, for washing clothes and dishes. You may wonder what detergent has to do with pollution and wild life, but the fact is detergents and disinfectants don't just vanish after being used. They go down the drains, and then through sewage plants, and into rivers, and finally into the sea. Somebody, somewhere, on the way along, has to deal with them. Some disinfectants break down to harmless products, but too much kills the bacteria which help to purify sewage. Detergents may pass through the sewage works without being decomposed, and cause great masses of foam in rivers, called 'detergent swans'. Today most detergents are what are known as 'soft' detergents, and they are broken down more easily, but they can still do damage. They contain a lot of phosphate, which is needed in plant nutrition, but too much of it upsets the plant balance in rivers and lakes. It may then cause 'algal bloom' – great blankets of scum on top of the water. Sewage is purified and made safe, in most cases, before being discharged into rivers, but it also adds nitrate to the water. Then nitrates and phosphates work together to cause over-enrichment, called *eutrophication*. This may produce even more algal growth, causing fish to suffocate. Here is a perfect example of a long chain of happenings in nature set off without harmful intention.

Sometimes we are tempted to overdo the whole business of pest control in the house, in an effort to deal with problems before they arise. If we use aerosols, vapour strips, disinfectants, sprays, moth proofing, fly repellents, and all the other methods of keeping pests at bay, and if we use them regularly as preventives rather than as cures, we may cause quite a build up of poison, particularly in small houses and kitchens. This can be harmful to human beings and also to household pets. If any substance is *killing* to any one form of life, such as fly spray, it may be *harmful* to others without actually killing them. In the house all pesticides based on organochlorines should be avoided, that is, those containing D.D.T., dieldrin, or lindane. Those containing pyrethrum or derris are safer, and the contents should be listed on the container. Too much D.D.T. and other long-lasting poisons have already been let loose in the world.

There are other ways in which household action can help in dealing with world-wide problems. As modern life grows more complicated, we use far more of everything in the home, not just food, but industrial commodities of all kinds. An example is paper. The world is swallowing paper at a tremendous rate, and paper comes from trees. Every year nearly 200 million tons of wood are used for paper. A single issue of the American *New York Times* uses wood covering 190 acres of forest. Once gone, these majestic forest trees have gone for hundreds of years, with the food, shelter, and protection they give to many species of life; new forests *may* grow, but in some cases regeneration may be impossible. It may seem a small thing, but if waste paper could be collected, and re-used, this would be a real contribution to the problem of world conservation. For the same reason, and also because supplies are running short, many other materials and metals should be re-cycled whenever possible.

43

Water is a precious commodity, and one we tend to use quite unthinkingly. We each use about 90 gallons a day, and this figure is rising rapidly, as more and more people want more and more water. All industrial processes are greedy water users. Up to 100,000 gallons of water may be used in making a single car. So more reservoirs have to be constructed, again involving much loss of land available for wild life, and destruction of habitats. A well-known example is the reservoir at Cow Green, in Upper Teesdale, to meet the industrial needs of Teesside. Many acres of the most beautiful moorland have gone for ever, and there may be quite incalculable effects on a wide surrounding area, although it is one of the most interesting botanical sites in the world, with unique associations of plants.

As it happens, the industrial use of water is so much greater than domestic use that economy in the home does not help much. But the time may come when our drinking water will come to us, like milk, in bottles, and a much lower standard of purity have to be accepted for other purposes, in the interests of water economy. In the meantime, other forms of water supply such as the desalination of sea water, or the construction of barrages across areas like the Wash or Morecambe Bay, will have to be explored, and some assessment made of the damage they in their turn might do to wild life habitats.

4

THE GARDEN OF A NATURALIST

EVERY GARDEN A NATURE RESERVE

THERE are twenty times more blackbirds in gardens than on farm land. In an area of houses and small gardens in north London it was found that 21 kinds of birds were able to live and breed there, in addition to those just visiting. Many former woodland birds have adapted themselves to garden conditions, including chaffinches, thrushes, great tits and blue tits, hedge sparrows, and wrens. Fifty different birds are now fairly regular visitors to bird tables for winter feeding. In gardens too you can often find butterflies, such as the cabbage white, small tortoiseshell, peacock, red admiral, and painted lady. So as the area of real countryside in Britain grows less and less, and as conditions on agricultural land become less favourable to wild life, gardens are becoming increasingly valuable as places of shelter for Britain's flora and fauna. A good slogan for the naturalist is, '*Every garden a nature reserve*'.

Regrettably there are three factors that make gardens less useful than they might be. These are cats, the excessive use of pesticides and sprays, and the over-enthusiastic gardener. Cats cause tremendous bird losses, far more than oil pollution at sea, although this gets much more publicity. Usually the birds can make up their own losses, but in certain places cats may prevent birds from

45

breeding at all, as they destroy the nests. The best that can be done against them is to site feeding tables and nesting boxes well out of their reach, keep them indoors at the main bird feeding times, or keep a dog, who will at any rate chase your neighbours' cats out of the garden. Chemicals in the garden are even more damaging than cats. A well-known advertisement in gardening magazines bears the message, 'Your garden is a battlefield', and urges warfare on all fronts against pests such as aphids, slugs, snails, insects of all kinds, many birds, and all weeds. But the naturalist-gardener welcomes many different forms of life because they are interdependent. Without nettles and other weeds there will be few butterflies, because many of the larvae require them for their food. Without insects there will be few birds. An interesting garden will contain many other things besides beds of prize-winning flowers, fruit and vegetables. But all forms of wild life want to be left alone. They need privacy, security, and freedom from disturbance. So the gardener who is always tidying, hoeing, raking, sweeping, mowing, weeding, and burning, is the greatest pest of all. Much of the wild life interest of a garden comes as a bonus to the lazy gardener.

WILD LIFE GARDENING

Lawns and areas of grass have much more to offer birds if they are not over-treated with weed-killer and worm-killer, and if the grass is left slightly longer than the perfectionist might wish. The soil will then remain full of living creatures. From about a square foot of turf and soil you can float out in water about 100 creatures visible to the naked eye, including worms, caterpillars, leather-jackets, grubs, slugs, spiders, centipedes, woodlice, beetles and others, quite apart from the wonderful microscopic worlds also to be found in soil. Again, weed-free

46

turf is much less interesting and attractive than a lawn containing white clover, yarrow, thyme, and camomile, as well as daisies, dandelions, and buttercups. The larvae of many butterflies feed on grasses, including the meadow brown, ringlet, small heath, grayling, wall, small copper, common blue, and small skipper butterflies, though you would be very fortunate to see many of these in your garden. At one time lawns were thought of as mosaics of colour, not smooth green linoleum. If this does not appeal to the gardener, perhaps odd corners of rough grass could be left, or strips along the edge. It has even been suggested that in a square or rectangular piece of lawn the gardener should mow the middle in a circle, so that the corners are left rough. These might then contain the 'weeds' listed, plus flowers from the hayfield such as lady's smock and meadow sweet, as well as naturalized bulbs, and wild scabious, bugle, ragwort, poppies, and mallow, all of which are attractive to butterflies. If one patch is left really wild and uncut, along the foot of a hedge, you will find there birds, slugs, and snails, and perhaps a hedgehog.

A free-growing mixed hedge kept tidy rather than clipped will give birds food, shelter, and nesting sites. The best kinds of shrubs are hawthorn, common privet (allowed to flower), spindle, elder, yew, and holly, with honeysuckle and ivy growing among them. One or two wild crab apples or wild pears will add to the food supply. If there is room, taller trees will act as song posts for birds, and native kinds such as oak or ash, or smaller ones such as mountain ash, are more useful than ornamental flowering cherries. Hazel nuts, or walnuts, will bring squirrels. Ivy should not be removed from trees, because it does not damage healthy trees, and if left to grow old and thick it provides very good nesting places, while the flower, coming late in the autumn, attracts bees and butterflies. Piles of dead leaves left under trees are homes for many insects, so that blackbirds will be seen rummaging through them for food later in the year. Piles of old logs, in damp corners, will house woodlice and grubs, and in autumn or warm wet winters there will be fungi growing there. Old apple trees are beloved by birds, and may bring such visitors as redwings in winter. Dropped pears attract butterflies, especially when the fruit is rotten and slightly fermented, and the stumps of old trees are invaluable for both insects and birds. Under the loose bark of rotting trees there will be more insects, and any holes will be used by cavity-nesting birds. Berries from the Christmas mistletoe may germinate on apple trees if you keep them until February or March, and then squeeze them into small cracks in the bark, preferably on the underside of branches where they cannot be washed off by rain. It is best to plant as many seeds as you can, because only a few, if any, will grow, and you are more likely to get male and female plants, both of which are needed for pollination.

When beds of perennial or annual flowers are being planted, great favourites with butterflies are honesty, sweet rocket, aubretia, arabis, and polyanthus. Later in the year Michaelmas daisies and the ice plant (*Sedum spectabile*) are often covered with butterflies. Sunflowers attract finches, and if some of the heads are kept and dried, the seeds will be useful for feeding birds throughout the winter. It is usual for gardeners to try to tidy their gardens in autumn, taking off all the dead flowers, and removing plants that have finished their season; but if it is a hard winter, the dead heads of Michaelmas daisies, dahlias, and many other plants, give welcome shelter to birds, particularly against wind.

A large old garden with many different trees and shrubs in it, as well as neglected corners and perhaps a pond, is bound to have many natural attractions for all sorts of wild life. It will even have many small habitats worth looking at. An old garden wall, protected from the wind and warmed by the sun, will be adopted by birds and butterflies. The older and more ruined it is, the better. Nooks and crannies will be filled with wallflowers, sweet rocket, and other rockery plants. If the odd brick or stone has fallen out, behind ivy or roses or winter jasmine, you may find robins, wagtails, or spotted flycatchers nesting there. The compost heap will have a rich insect and small animal population, and on warm sunny evenings flycatchers will hover above it. Even the waterbutt is interesting, for dragonflies, water lilies, and minnows may be found there. Old bonfire sites often have strange plants growing on them, from seeds in household refuse (melons, tomatoes, and sweet corn). There is even a special moss associated with bonfire sites, the fire moss.

An old garden shed – best of all, a wooden one – is most useful. In winter peacock and small tortoiseshell butterflies may hibernate there, as in the house. Swallows, blackbirds, and robins will nest under shelves and ledges. Wrens will use any old corner. One naturalist has suggested leaving an old tweed coat hanging in the shed, in case a robin should wish to nest in the pocket. The door of the shed should be left open, or a large hole left somewhere in the roof, as an escape route for a startled bird. Tawny owls will sometimes nest in apple barrels placed high up, perhaps in the corner of the roof, the opening being flush with the wall and the barrel itself fastened securely on the inside wall. A blackbird once chose as a nesting site a corner behind one of the rungs of a ladder leaning against a wall. Unfortunately the bird was confused by the similarity of the different rungs, and was so baffled that it laid nest foundations in every one of them. Later it tried to build up three of the foundations, but was never able to finish any one of them, presumably exhausted mentally and physically by the hard work put in.

A new garden without these attractions of old trees, walls, sheds, and ponds, needs more management if it is to be attractive to wild life. A winter feeding table for birds will be necessary, as there is bound to be less growing food available until the garden is well established. Nesting boxes for different types of bird will also be needed, in default of thick foliage; and a bird bath will be equally necessary. If possible, even the smallest garden should have a tiny wilderness in it. A briar rose, or hawthorn, planted in a corner at the bottom of the garden, could be underplanted with wild flowers. Chaffinches, green finches, and even gold finches can be attracted by the seed of knotgrass, groundsel, plantains, shepherd's purse, and charlock. Thistles grown in an old bucket with holes punched in the bottom, one or two teazle plants, or docks allowed to flower, will add to the value of such a corner. A small patch of nettles in a quiet

THE GARDEN OF A NATURALIST

1. OAK TREE WITH NESTING HOLE
2. IVY FOR NESTING BIRDS
3. MICHAELMAS DAISIES
4. SUNFLOWERS
5. COMPOST HEAP
6. NEST BOX
7. SHED WITH DOOR LEFT OPEN FOR NESTING BIRDS
8. MOUNTAIN ASH TREE
9. CRAB APPLE
10. MIXED HEDGE
11. NETTLES
12. ROUGH GRASS
13. BIRD FEEDING TABLE
14. POND

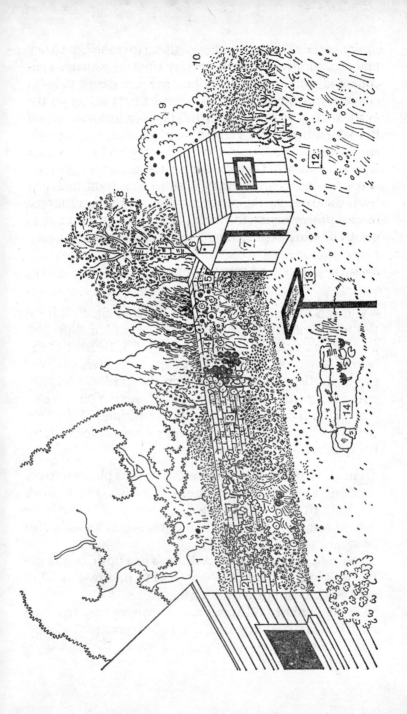

sunny corner will allow the small tortoiseshell, peacock and red admiral butterflies to lay their eggs there. Peacock and small tortoiseshell butterflies lay eggs in large clusters, but the red admiral fixes its eggs singly on the nettle leaves, and each caterpillar folds a leaf round itself to make a little tent. Fresh young nettles are constantly needed, so it is advisable to cut down part of the nettle area from time to time, to permit new growth. If you are very tidy-minded, you may wish to screen off this area from the main garden, with a hedge, or trellis, or screen of decorative concrete blocks, and this can be used to grow climbing plants, in which birds may nest.

MAKE A GARDEN NATURE TRAIL

Whatever your garden is like – old or new, large or small – you can make a nature trail in it. In its simplest form this means planning a route round the garden with signposts or notices indicating points of interest for the benefit of visitors. What these points are, and how many there can be, depends entirely on the garden, and they may change at different times in the year. You can also make a map of the garden at different times of the year to show what seasonal changes take place on your nature trail. Here are some suggestions:

1. Any features of natural interest, such as plants or trees specially interesting in themselves, or attractive to birds or butterflies, for instance a buddleia (liked by butterflies), a sedum (the same) or a honeysuckle (for bees).

2. Any old bird's nest – a blackbird's in a bush, or a house martin's in the eaves, or a blue tit's in a nesting-box – but not before breeding is over for the season.

3. A maximum and minimum thermometer, recorded each day, and a rain gauge, also to be recorded each day, and a sundial.

4. A small collection of any odd objects found in the garden – interesting stones, any fossils (the kind called the devil's toe nails is often found), bits of clay pipe, feathers or eggshells dropped by birds, fragments of old pottery, any bones found in the garden, of mice, voles, or birds, or any pieces of an old wasps' nest. Old keys and old nails often turn up. You will be very unlucky if you never find anything like this in your garden.

5. Any plants, trees or shrubs grown from cuttings, with a note of the place where they were obtained, the variety, and the date of planting.

6. A section of a tree made into a seat or a table, with a notice saying what kind of tree it is, and its age calculated from the rings.

7. Any old farming or agricultural tools you may be able to rescue, or a piece of old basketry such as an eel basket or duck's decoy nest, or an old lobster pot.

8. A flat irregular stone, with snails shells on it, to serve as an anvil for thrushes to break open snail shells.

9. Any tree with a witches' broom on it – that is, a thickening, or growth caused by a gall. It may look like a squirrel's nest, rather large and untidy.

10. Lichens and mosses wherever they occur.

11. A pile of seashells, collected on holiday, or attractive pebbles from the beach.

12. Trees, shrubs, or nettles with larvae on them with identification where possible.

13. Specially exotic plants, such as *Metasequoia*, a tree known as a fossil, but once believed to be extinct, although it has now been rediscovered.

14. A labelled collection of fur, feathers, and bones from birds, animals or fish such as pheasants, chickens, ducks, rabbits, or hares, bought as food in the house. Pheasants' feathers are especially beautiful. A fishmonger with a game licence is often able to give them away.

15. A Christmas tree planted out when the Christmas decorations are taken down in the house, with a note of when it was planted.

These are only a few of the many possibilities. The chief considerations are careful labelling, so that the visitor knows exactly what he is looking at, and variety.

5

MAKE A MINI NATURE RESERVE

IT is not essential to have a large garden and lots of space to create a nature reserve. With some ingenuity very tiny areas can be converted into interesting sanctuaries. Plans may have to be scaled down to match the resources available, but the only real necessities are light and air.

Experiments can be made in corners of gardens and yards, and in narrow flower beds along walls. An angle corner between two walls is easiest to start with, but assuming a space two feet wide and about six feet long, at the foot of a wall, something can be done, whether in a garden or yard, or on a terrace or balcony. Disadvantages of one sort or another may turn out to be plus factors. A bright sunny place will enable plants to grow well, and this will encourage butterflies, but a darker damp area will suit toads, snails, ferns, and fungi. Many of the suggestions already made for garden management can be adopted in miniature. A little experience of a particular site and its potentialities will soon show what the long-term possibilities will be. If the space available is overlooked by a window, so much the better, as it can then be observed from inside. Opposite the kitchen window is a good idea, but sometimes a landing window or one in an upstairs room will give a better view.

If your mini nature reserve can be placed against a wall or on the side of a wooden shed, the first thing to do is to establish creepers growing up the wall or on a trellis. (If no background wall is available, a firmly fixed trellis has advantages.) Crowd the creepers together for maximum effect, and if possible use native creepers such as honeysuckle, ivy, convolvulus, bryony, and the wild clematis or old man's beard. Honeysuckle turns in a clockwise direction, whereas convolvulus climbs anti-clockwise. You will soon be able to see this for yourself. Many of these will grow from seed. One of the best is the ordinary wild bramble, or even a cultivated blackberry if you can bring yourself to leave the fruit for wild life instead of eating it yourself. If the wall behind is an old one, poke little plants into various crevices, such as the ivy-leaved toadflax (any friend living in the country should be able to give you a bit to start with, and when it has really got going you will be able to give rooted pieces of it to other people) or grow stonecrop or moss. Garden flowers are often easier to establish than wild ones – aubretia, alyssum or soapwort will all grow in cascades down your wall. If nails can be driven into the wall, hang a tit nesting box five or six feet high, preferably with some shelter from one of the creepers, or an old kettle, tipped backwards, with one or two holes punched in it to let the rain run away. Robins may nest there, and they have been known to do so in old two-pound syrup tins treated in the same way. Even an old boot hanging up may be used. An old-fashioned broom made of twigs, standing on its handle, or a bundle of pea sticks, may attract some other small bird to nest. A row of artificial nests for house martins can be put under the eaves of a garden shed. Keep an eye on such nesting places from a distance. Inspection may cause birds to desert. Other nails will support hanging baskets of plants, a bag of feathers or moss for birds to use when nesting, or seed hoppers with wild bird seed in them.

If there is soil at the foot of your wall, plant sunflowers at the back, or climbing nasturtiums to grow into your creepers. Nearer to the front, put marigolds, cornflowers, Shirley poppies, clarkia, mignonette, and candytuft, with aubretia and alyssum in front. Some of these are best grown from seed, as annuals. You do not need more than two or three of each, and they should be placed fairly close together. If you are using a paved area, some of them will grow in pots or tubs, kept watered. Petunias and geraniums are fashionable but have less interest for butterflies than less flamboyant flowers, although the ordinary red geranium is sometimes visited by them. Roses of the modern kind are useless for attracting butterflies. A small buddleia bush is worth a place, and there is a dwarf garden variety called Border Beauty. Other plants to grow in pots are hyssop (another magnet for butterflies) and almost any herb, including borage, lavender, or chives allowed to flower. As already suggested for the garden wilderness, plants such as thistles, nettles and mint are best grown in buckets, tucked among the flowers. Also tucked among them you can have a pile of stones, or old tiles to attract mosses and lichens. A damp rotting log, or tree stump, kept wet, will harbour larvae, grubs, woodlice, and fungi, just as in the bigger garden. An upturned plant pot, resting on a piece of tile, may bring a toad or snails. A raw potato under a piece of damp sacking will be discovered by some small creatures. If it is placed on soil you will find snails, centipedes, or ants there, and certainly woodlice. Snails and slugs can be bred successfully in small enclosures. If space allows, you can experiment with pitfall traps – jam-jars set in the ground, either empty or baited with fish meat, or fruit, to attract tiny animals. A collection of mosses, or a fern garden, will add interest. A flowering wall made up of hollow breeze blocks has endless possibilities, or you can have a peat wall built up out of blocks of peat bought at a gardeners' supply shop. Both of these can be as big or as small as you wish. You may be able to exploit the possibilities of roof gardening on your shed – roof gardening in the sense of growing plants such as houseleeks actually on the roof surface. A tiny rock garden at the foot of your flowering wall completes the picture, or if this is not possible, many rock plants will grow in gravel or scree, or between paving stones.

HOW TO ATTRACT BIRDS

Some further provision is needed for birds. You already have some nesting sites, and seeds growing to attract tits and finches. Drinking water for them can be provided in a bird-bath, preferably shallow and not too elaborate. A dustbin lid resting on three bricks is often recommended. A baking tin will do, or an old frying-pan, or a shallow flowerpot of the kind with no hole in the bottom, or one of the plastic trays now sold for gardeners. In summer birds will drink and splash there, so if you place the container carefully among your plants the birds will do your watering for you. Clean fresh water is needed every two or three days. Try to see that the drinking water is not underneath the feeding table, or much food will be lost there. A similar receptacle for use as a dusting area is also needed. Again a dustbin lid will do, full of coarse sand mixed with fine gravel or soil and occasionally changed to remove any insect parasites. These may include various fleas, lice and mites and are themselves worth looking at. A broom handle driven into the soil, or placed upright in a large plant pot of stone and soil, will hold a bird table. A small wooden tray is as good as anything, or you can nail a crossbar on to the broom handle and hang on it bags of peanuts, pieces of fat from the butcher, seed hoppers, or cartons of fat melted down and poured over breadcrumbs. If many birds are attracted, small experiments in feeding can be made. Try sunflower seeds, hemp, coarse suet, oatmeal, rice pudding, cheese, bacon rind, strings of peanuts (blue tits soon learn to pull them up and hold them in position while they eat), apples, cooked potatoes (starlings like them peeled) but not porridge (too sticky on the feathers), currants, or too much bread. Dried coconut should never be given as it may swell up inside the bird. All this is for winter feeding. At other times of year there is usually plenty of food about for birds, but they will use the water and dust baths at all times. Nuts and fat can be put out for tits at all times of the year, but in spring and summer it is more for fun than actual feeding. Bird canteens, snack bars, tit bells, suet logs, and many other devices for feeding birds are available, but perfectly good ones can be made at home. Plastic garden netting of various sizes, made into tubes and tacked on to a wooden base can be used. String bags, or nets such as those used by greengrocers for carrots or oranges, are easy to fill and hang. Remember that if you start feeding birds in a hard winter, you are obliged to go on doing so, because the birds become dependent on you.

For amusement only there are many other things you can do. A mirror hanging on the wall interests birds, and you may see them posturing and displaying there, but if it seems to frighten them, or cause them to dash against it as if attacking an enemy, take it away immediately. A water garden, however small, or a tiny fishpond, with the smallest possible fountain, would be great additions, but visiting cats and dogs may be interested in them too.

Make a Chart of Visits to the Bird Table

Time of Day	Nuts	Fat	Seeds	Bread	Water
7.00 – 7.30					
7.30 – 8.00					
8.00 – 8.30					
8.30 – 9.00					
9.30 – 10.00					
10.00 – 10.30					
And so on throughout the day.					

Write in the names of birds you see visiting food and water at the time they arrive. If possible, put in brackets the greatest number seen at any one time, e.g. 8.00 – 8.30 Bluetits (9).

In a country garden or even in the suburbs water often attracts foxes.

All sorts of containers for plants and other material can be used. Strawberry barrels save space. Stone sinks and urns are decorative, but old baskets, pans, and crocks have their uses. Three-tiered cakestands, vegetable racks, or tall pan racks, can all be used to great advantage as they will support creepers as well as shelves full of odd-ments. Even an old hatstand can be incorporated, be-cause of its different levels. An old wheelbarrow, especially the sturdy wooden kind, can itself hold a com-plete zoological display. Some of these objects may have a conservation interest of their own, as cottage antiques or 'bygones', such as old wooden butter churns or dolly tubs. Junk shops often have oddments that don't qualify as valuable antiques but have an interest as fragments of the past. In a modern setting, structures of concrete blocks, or decorative white plastic trellis, can be made to give a unity to the display area as a whole.

The ideas sketched here are only starting points. The enthusiast and the specialist will soon wish to do more. An outdoor *vivarium* for toads, frogs, or lizards, ac-cording to interests and circumstances, has a very special appeal. A tiny *arboretum* is a talking point – that is, a collection of trees grown from cuttings or seeds such as chestnuts, acorns, beech mast, lime seeds or haws. Most of these are best collected as seed in the autumn, kept in damp sand during the winter, and planted in spring. Trees such as willows grow well and quickly from cut-tings. The keeping of bees is a subject in itself, and a fascinating one, but there is equal interest in keeping and breeding ants, wasps, snails, slugs, and worms. The scope is unlimited. The important consideration is that wherever you live you can surround yourself with living things. And as you will want your plants and animals to flourish, you will soon find out their likes and dislikes and how their needs can best be met either in these limited surroundings or in the wider world beyond your garden gate.

If you can do absolutely nothing else, at least in winter hang half a coconut outside a window. Even the housewife shaking the table cloth in the yard is to some extent a conservationist.

6

WILD LIFE IN THE WINDOW

A WINDOW-SILL can be a wonderful place for the naturalist and his specimens, because it is so easy to see what is going on there, and so much can be learnt from close acquaintance with various forms of life.

WINDOW GARDENING

Easiest and best known of the various possibilities is window gardening. Apart from exotic house plants, and indoor bulbs such as daffodils and hyacinths (the latter most interesting when grown in hyacinth glasses, to show the roots) you can grow mustard and cress on damp flannel or blotting paper, little gardens of carrot and beet tops in saucers of water, pineapple tops in an inch of soil kept well-watered, and little fruit trees from orange, lemon, or grapefruit pips, or from peach and plum stones. Try slicing an inch off the root end of a carrot, scooping out a hollow space inside the carrot, and hanging it upside down by means of a wire handle. If you keep the carrot filled with water the crown will sprout new green leaves which will find their own way to grow upwards in response to light. The stones of avocado pears are more difficult, but you may get one to germinate if you put it in a wine glass so that the base touches water, and then keep it warm. Another method is to plant the stone in soil and then keep it slightly moist and damp. In either case germination is very slow. Empty coconut shells make good containers for hanging gardens in the window-sill. Ivy seedlings in them with nasturtiums look well, or morning glory, or old man's beard, grown in soil or John Innes compost from a garden shop.

A tiny herb garden might contain *chives* (buy or beg a small clump), *mint* (from a small rooted cutting – apple or eau de cologne mint are good kinds), *parsley* (from seed), *sage* (also from seed) and *lavender* (buy a clump of a dwarf kind or grow a cutting in sandy soil). If space is limited, the smaller herbs such as thyme can be grown in a small strawberry barrel, with violets, wild straw-berries, or saxifrages, in other pockets, or any other wild plants not too big to grow in this way.

Even more interesting botanically is using your widow-sill as a nursery for wild flower seeds. Germination is often very variable, and some of the most familiar plants are more difficult than others, requiring special conditions of soil. In most cases seeds can be collected in the late summer, kept dry in separate labelled plastic bags, and then grown in John Innes compost in the spring. Egg boxes are useful for the seeds, but prick them out into larger containers when grown into seedlings. Yoghourt cartons are the right size, with holes in the bottom for drainage. After a country walk try any unknown seeds you have picked up, in trouser turn ups or in mud on the soles of shoes. Otherwise try violets, poppies, vetch, forget-me-nots, or whatever takes your fancy if you can get the ripe seeds without doing damage or causing loss to a wild habitat.

Another idea for your window is a mould garden. Get a clear plastic box and put in it scraps of bread, orange peel, a bit of leather from an old shoe, a piece of cake, and any other such oddments. Give everything a good spray (the garden should be moist but not watery), cover the box with a piece of clean plastic to keep it moist, and examine it from time to time to see what it looks and smells like.

MAKING A TERRARIUM

A shady indoor window-sill is ideal for a *terrarium* – a miniature garden enclosed in glass. Almost any clear glass container will do – a goldfish bowl, a glass goblet (not coloured glass) or any plain glass dish. A jam-jar is not quite the right shape. Best of all is a clean polished brandy glass. Line the bottom of it with any moss, green side out, and bring some of the moss a little way up the side. On top of the moss, in the little cup you have constructed, put a little leaf-mould or John Innes compost. Then with tweezers make a tiny garden using the smallest plants and rooted cuttings you can get hold of, such as moss, tiny ferns, scraps of rock plants, of different heights, with three or four evergreen seedlings. Cacti won't do as they need drier conditions than your terrarium. Spray or sprinkle with rain water, put a sheet of plain glass over the top, and leave it alone. Lift the top occasionally, to enjoy the smell and to give the plants air, and keep the garden damp but not soggy, as in the case of your mould garden. Everything must be on a small scale, with a variety of shape, colour, and height. A pebble or shell will give added interest. A fascinating small world can be created in this way, and needs practically no attention for months.

PLANTING A MOSS GARDEN

To make a moss garden for your window-sill, you need a large plate, such as a soup plate, with a rim round, or a large tin plate of the kind used by campers. A flat baking tin will do, but as it may rust and mark the paint, it will either have to be painted or kept on a waterproof plastic tray. An aquarium tank is also possible, and in this case to keep the mosses damp a glass sheet can be placed over the top. Sprinkle gravel on the bottom of your container, and then a thin layer of soil, or rotten leaf mould, or compost. The mosses to collect in gardens and from walls include silver thread moss (about an inch high, and with shiny silvery tufts), wall screw moss (much smaller, and very common along the tops of walls, or on ridges and tiles), common cord moss and beard moss. In towns you find moss in damp places such as the sides of grates, under downspouts, at the end of gutters, and on garden walls. In damp woodlands there are many other kinds – bank hair moss, lesser fork moss, juniper-leaved hair moss, silky fork moss, white fork moss, common hair moss. You will find them among trees, on rotten logs, on the edges of paths, or at the foot of gate posts. The moss garden should be kept damp, but not in water. Use a scent spray or a sprinkler top on a bottle. If you are successful, the plants may produce stems bearing tiny capsules, from which new plants eventually develop when in natural conditions. Rotten wood and twigs are useful among your plants. Really wet areas such as the margins of ponds, ditches, and bogs, produce quite different kinds of moss. The best known is bog moss, or sphagnum, much used by florists because it holds water so well, and can be used to keep other plants damp or even to grow seeds in. You can usually buy bits of it from a florist's shop. Then you can make sphagnum balls about the size of tennis balls, tying them with string to keep them in shape, and leaving one end of the string to hang up each ball. After the balls have been well soaked in water you can push seeds into them and then hang them up. If you can keep them damp the seeds will germinate. The easiest seeds are garden seeds such as nasturtiums, alyssum, virginia stock, or candytuft, but try ivy or honeysuckle. A sponge can be used instead of the sphagnum moss.

A WINDOW BOX FOR BIRDS

Of course you cannot keep any kind of birds on your window-sill – many naturalists are sorry to see *any* birds kept in captivity, even canaries, or budgerigars, and wild birds are out of the question. But there is one way of bringing birds *almost* into the picture. Get or make a nesting box such as those made for tits, and take off the back. Then fit the box on to the outside of the window, so that the back is against the glass, and any bird using it has complete freedom of coming and going without entering the window. On the *inside* of the window, fix a square of cardboard covering the pane of glass behind the box. If the nesting box is taken over by a bird – a blue tit, a robin, or even a sparrow – you can gradually remove or slide away the cardboard on the inside, and if you are careful the bird will not be frightened away, so that you can watch the nest being constructed, the eggs laid and hatched, and the young ones fed.

You may not be lucky enough to get a bird nesting there, but you can increase the chances if you put bird food near it during the winter, so that the birds become accustomed to approaching the window. A piece of fat dangling below will attract blue tits. A robin can be enticed by meal worms. Indeed robins delight in meal worms at any time, and can often be persuaded to eat them from an outstretched hand. They are not worms, but the larvae of a beetle, and you can easily buy them from a pet dealer, or you can breed your own, on your window-sill. Buy half an ounce of them live, to start you off, and put them on a three inch layer of bran (also from the pet shop) at the bottom of a biscuit tin. Put in half a raw potato or carrot, and a little crumbled dog biscuit. A sheet of perforated zinc over the top of the container is a good idea. The meal worms bury themselves in the bran. They will turn into pupae, and then into adult beetles, which will again deposit eggs. Change the potato or carrot from time to time, and add more bran every week or so if needed. The box needs to be cleaned out completely every three months. To sort out the larvae, pupae, and adult worms from the bran to be discarded, simply shake the contents of your box on to a newspaper through the zinc cover, and then put them into fresh bran. Take two or three meal worms for robin whenever you walk round the garden.

IDEAS FOR MINI ZOOS

A very sunny window will not do for an *aquarium*, but if a place can be found that does not have too much sun, and does not get too hot, there are various kinds to be considered. The most natural kind is the simplest and the most interesting to watch. Get an ordinary rectangular glass aquarium tank, and then on a warm spring day visit a fairly shallow pond. Try to find one that has plenty of vegetation growing round it, and one with banks that are not too steep. Skim the surface of the water with a plankton net (this is finer than an ordinary fishing net, and can be made at home from a nylon stocking) collecting the visible surface animals and the microscopic animals and plants. Do this several times, emptying the catch into a large polythene bottle, and then three-quarters fill the bottle with pond water. Then do the same with an ordinary fishing net through the middle depths of the pond, as far as you can reach, again putting your catch into a bottle and three-quarters filling it. Then with a trowel scoop up some of the mud from the bottom of the pond, again putting it in a bottle, plenty of it, and adding pond water. Take some of the rooted plants from the middle and bottom depths of the pond, choosing different kinds and different heights, for variety. Then when you reach home simply transfer all you have got carefully into your tank, rooting the plants in the mud when it has settled. Ideally you should sieve out all the animals, fish, and larvae, keeping them in pond water overnight until the mud in the tank has settled and you can put the plants in first. Then you can also have a look at your catch with a magnifying glass. Feed with small quantities of proprietary fish food, try to keep the water clear, remove any dead animals, and avoid the large water beetle as it eats the other creatures.

Your haul will vary considerably at different times and in different places. The season, temperature, flow of water, and nature of the soil, all have their effects. You may find you have many aquatic larvae, such as those of the caddis fly, mayfly, and dragonfly, or of several other species. There may be water spiders, mites, pond snails, freshwater mussels, fish such as sticklebacks and minnows, and all sorts of other things such as flatworms, roundworms, leeches, water fleas, water lice, freshwater shrimps, water boatmen, and water scorpions. Your plants may include algae and liverworts, and others such as water violet, starwort, water crowfoot, and frogbit. If you cannot visit a pond, all you need can be bought at special aquarist shops, and you can get expert advice there, but on the whole the hit-or-miss method is more interesting. An aquarium of native British species of fish, animals, and plants will be at least as interesting as one of tropical fish.

In the same sort of way you can set up a bog or swamp garden, using a shallow earthenware pot or a large baking tin. Fill it with the mud, decaying vegetation, soil, water and animals from the *edge* of the pond, planting some of the smaller plants found there. This will be a different collection from that found in the pond itself, and it should be wet rather than actually in water. Again it will vary enormously according to the type of pond you find.

A *vivarium* is rather different. A container can be bought, or one made from a large box. If you use a box, one side should be replaced by a glass front, and a cover with air holes (or a sheet of perforated zinc) will also be needed. Frogs and toads need moist conditions. Damp earth or moss on the floor, and a pie dish of water, will be needed, and the animals should be fed on live insects, meal worms, slugs, and earthworms. A few small rocks and one or two small ferns or clumps of grass are useful. Lizards from a pet shop need drier warmer conditions. Sand, rocks, a dish of water, and sunshine, are their main requirements. On the whole, a larger vivarium constructed outside offers more scope for keeping these sorts of creatures.

Your window-sill collection can well include a captive spider. The ordinary hairy house spider can be kept in a clear plastic food box with a small hiding-place in it such as an open-ended carboard tube or little open-ended box glued down one side, and maybe a small twig. The spider will soon begin to spin a web and will then feed if you drop the occasional live fly into the box. From time to time the spider will cast its skin, and may live a year or more without much attention. You'll have to remove the bodies of the flies from time to time, as the spider doesn't actually eat them but sucks juices from them.

Not everybody likes spiders, so what about a *wormery*? This is very easy and amusing to watch. Make a cylinder of clear perspex (or a glass jam-jar with the bottom removed – you can do this by pouring boiling water into it, carefully) stand it on a plant pot of soil, and fill it with alternate layers of dark soil and light-coloured sand. Sprinkle a little grass seed on the top layer and keep the contents slightly damp. Put ten or a dozen worms in the plant pot and watch what happens over the next few days. A strip of black paper clipped on one side of the cylinder can be marked with the original position of the different layers of soil and sand. As there are 30 different species of worms in Britain, you may find different kinds behaving in different ways. Worth watching.

The construction of a *formicarium* or ant-palace is more complicated but even more interesting. There are many different methods, and experience will suggest the best way. The simplest is to take two old photograph frames, about 12 by 8 inches, with the glass in but without backs. Glue them together so that the two sheets of glass are about half an inch apart. Before gluing them gouge out a slit on one of the short sides, so that when placed together the shallow box you have made has this narrow slit as an opening. Screw the box down to a firm base so that it can't topple over, with the slit at the top. Put soil between the panes of glass, not quite to the top, and dab a little honey or golden syrup above the soil level. You then have to introduce your ants, before plugging the slit with cotton wool. Once there, the ants will soon start making roads and then their palace. The point of having a very thin container is that they show up more clearly against the glass. When not under observation the formicarium should be kept covered with a black cloth, and then preferably watched in artificial light which does not disturb them. A drop of honey every two or three days and a trickle of water, is all that will be required. But some hints are needed on collecting the ants to put them in your container. Find a colony in the garden, perhaps under a stone, of red ants (Myrmica). If you search until you find an ant scurrying about you can trace it to its home. Dig out as much of the

MAKING A FORMICARIUM

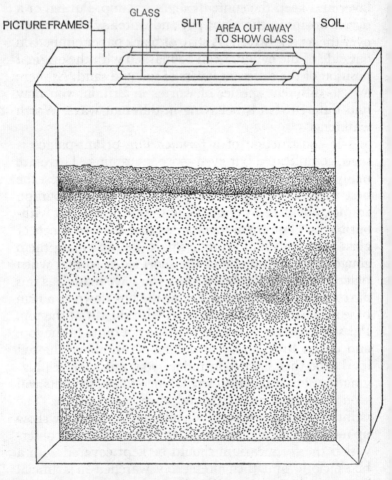

PICTURE FRAMES   GLASS   SLIT   AREA CUT AWAY TO SHOW GLASS   SOIL

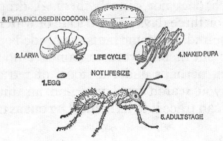

3. PUPA ENCLOSED IN COCOON

2. LARVA   LIFE CYCLE   4. NAKED PUPA

1. EGG   NOT LIFE SIZE

5. ADULT STAGE

colony as you can, with a large spade, in a solid cube if possible, and then on a white sheet carefully break off small pieces. Collect the ants in a bottle as they escape, taking about a hundred. Make sure you find a queen ant, recognizable as being much bigger than the others, and put her in a second bottle with half a dozen of the worker ants. Plug the bottles with cotton wool. Then replace the ant colony where you found it, and cover it with a stone. Worker ants will soon repair the damage. Introduce the ants and the queen into the formicarium through a paper funnel.

BUTTERFLY FARMING

Finally, the most fascinating and absorbing pursuit of all is butterfly farming. Here only the very simplest method is described. To go further demands very considerable knowledge and experience. First a rearing cage has to be constructed. Take a jam-jar (to be kept full of water), a square of plywood with a hole in the middle to lie on the jar, a cylinder of perspex to stand on the plywood, and a square of perforated zinc to lie on top of the cylinder. The food plant stands in the jam-jar of water, but is placed so that the stem is pushed through the hole in the plywood, the leaves remaining in the cylinder above. Next, we have to find the eggs of a suitable butterfly. On a warm sunny April day watch for a small tortoiseshell butterfly in a patch of nettles. When ready to lay her eggs, the female tortoiseshell finds the nettles, 'drums' with her feet on a leaf to make sure it is the right kind, and then lays a batch of eggs on the underside – from 50 to 200 of them, in a tight cluster. Cut off the stem of nettle bearing this leaf, and put it in the rearing cage. Very soon, in a few days, if it is warm, the eggs hatch, and you will find clusters of striped spiny caterpillars. After a few more days, if the caterpillars seem to

73

be feeding well, most of them should be removed and taken back to the nettle bed, leaving only two or three in the cage, feeding on the nettle. Every few days the nettle has to be replaced with a fresh piece of the plant. Take off the perforated lid, and snip off the leaf or leaves on which the caterpillars are feeding. Let these leaves with the caterpillars fall on to the plywood base, and put the fresh nettle stalk in position. The caterpillars will move on to it themselves. Occasionally the cylinder should be lifted and any debris swept off the plywood. At length each caterpillar will move to the wall of the cage and hang himself up by a tail-pad of silk, before changing to a chrysalis, and finally, if you are lucky, the butterfly itself appears, in June or July. Try to be at hand to watch the wonderful process when the butterfly emerges. Take off the zinc top, open the window, and let the butterfly go away into the garden. The most important considerations are enormous care in handling eggs or caterpillars, if they have to be touched; the right choice of food plant, and enough fresh food of this kind; and the right temperature and air.

BECOMING A CONSERVATIONIST

There are many other possibilities for wild life in the window, some of them much more complicated, and perhaps more suitable for laboratory work. All the suggestions made here deal with living specimens, because it is through handling living material that understanding of the living world is best reached. But you shouldn't keep any animals – spiders, fish, ants, or anything else – unless you are prepared to look after them. If you don't, you will soon find all your containers have turned into mortuaries, and thoughtless killing is the opposite of conservation.

In these various experiments, you are isolating

74

sections of nature's network for more detailed study – whether you are working on the reactions of plants to light, or the spatial requirements of fish, or the feeding habits of butterflies or ants. As soon as you begin to observe plants and animals, you are a *naturalist*. When you begin to think in terms of the relationships between them – what they eat, where they live, how they need each other – you may be surprised to hear it, but already you are an *ecologist*. When you go on to consider in what ways they can be protected, and their requirements best met, you are a *conservationist*.

7

STREET SCENE

CITIES and towns are not just concrete jungles. Even in
heavily built-up areas there are *some* forms of wild life.
In the middle of Amsterdam, there is a large heronry.
You can count dozens of nests in tall trees near the university. Hedgehogs abound in Berlin parks, and the
foundations of a church in Dublin are threatened by
badgers. In Britain, wherever you are, in a town or
country, street or lane, you are never very far from
nature. As an experiment, see whether you can find any
place, even in large busy shopping areas, where absolutely no form of natural life is visible except men and
women, cats and dogs. There are gardens, parks,
squares, playing-fields, car parks, and laybys. A step or
two in any direction will bring into view a pigeon strutt-
ing on the ground, a few sparrows on a telegraph wire or
roof, a gull soaring overhead, a fragment of moss at the
foot of a drain, or a plant of shepherd's purse or sow
thistle struggling in a gutter. This is because nature is
infinitely resourceful, being quick to seize on any available empty space. You can test this by leaving a seed box
of sterilized soil lying outside. Before very long seedlings
of some sort will colonize even that small empty space.
Or you can paint a part of a wall with some sticky liquid,
and see what seeds come floating by to stick fast to it.
Soldiers in the First World War reported that small

birds were nesting and breeding in no-man's-land – the strip of land between the trenches – even during periods of great disturbance. If man ceased to exist, all our cities and towns would soon be covered with some form of vegetation, with its accompanying birds, insects, and animals.

BIRDS IN TOWNS

The most successful adaptation to urban conditions is found in birds, and the most urban bird of all is the pigeon. The sort found in towns is not the wood pigeon of our fields and farms, but a descendant of the rock dove, and it has found the buildings and roofs of towns an admirable substitute for its former rocky habitats. Trafalgar Square, in London, has many thousands of them feeding there every day. So has St. Mark's Square, in Venice – a very different place, but just as convenient for pigeons. In many cities they have become a pest. They live in squares and streets, near docks, railway stations, embankments, and open air cafés, wherever people congregate and are willing to feed them. Notices at main line stations in London threaten fines for feeding pigeons, but people take no notice. A study of pigeons in Leeds showed that in winter they lived almost entirely on scraps, including bread, cake, chocolate, and anything else they were offered or could snatch. At other times they find more of their own food in fields and gardens. The most devoted lovers of nature would agree their numbers are far too great for cleanliness or comfort. Many different methods of keeping their numbers down, or getting rid of them entirely, have been tried without great success. It would be interesting to watch for them in different towns, to see how widely conditions vary, whether there are some towns without pigeons, which of the others suffer most, and why these differences occur.

The nuisance value of starlings in towns is just as great. This is another example of a too successful adaptation. Indeed the starling has shown itself to be marvellously good at survival. In America today there may be about 50 million starlings, and all of them are descended from a few dozen released in Central Park, New York, not so very long ago. In Britain, both in town and country, it seems that conditions for breeding success are just too favourable, and there are no powerful controls keeping the numbers down. Man's presence is a help, instead of a hindrance, to both pigeons and starlings. Even city lights favour them, by helping to raise the temperature and giving more hours of light. In central areas the noise of starlings often drowns the roar of traffic. Although their habit of roosting on trees and buildings in towns is a comparatively new one, seen in London only in the last fifty years, the birds are intensely conservative, using the same places regularly, and each having its allotted space. If one bird drops out, it may be days or weeks before the gap in the roosting line is filled. They perch about four inches apart, just within pecking distance.

Starlings are more spectacular than pigeons, because they fly together, literally thousands at a time. They fly over in the winter dusk, black against the sky, wheeling and turning, gathering together until they all make for their roosting places. There are millions of them in the air at once, in a late winter afternoon. Their biomass – the total weight of living matter they represent – is as great as that of many other species of birds put together. Mysterious objects observed on radar screens, over the east of England, at first thought to be invading aircraft, turned out to be massive flocks of starlings. They are noisy, aggressive, dirty birds, doing much harm in chimneys, gutters, and on the frontages of buildings. But they are very entertaining to study, quarrelling, mimicking other birds, and behaving like a dominant species, at any rate with other birds, although they fly away if man gets too close. Starlings and pigeons are not on the list of birds protected in Britain.

Much more welcome birds in towns, because less obtrusive, include *sparrows*, cheeky but wary; *black-headed gulls*, now a familiar winter sight scavenging in London and other towns, coming inland up rivers, streaming out in the late afternoon, towards reservoirs and estuaries for the night; and other birds more rarely seen, such as the *black redstart*, first attracted to bombed sites in towns. Two summer visitors are *swifts* and *house martins*. House martins build their characteristic nests of mud and clay on the walls of houses, just under the eaves. They stay in England from April to October. A martin's nest on a house is said to bring happiness, and martins sometimes nest in the same places from year to year. You can often spot where their nests are by droppings on pavements, underneath the nests, and this would make it easier, in a small country town or part of one, to do a survey establishing how many nests there are and how they are distributed. There would be more in certain streets than others, and they would thin out towards the centre. The distribution could be marked up on a street map. You might walk miles without seeing any, and then find several, near open spaces or watery places, as the birds need mud for their nests. A town with a river running through it would be more likely to have house martins than one without. In some places there are huge colonies of these birds.

FLORA AND FAUNA IN STREETS

While your eyes are on the ground, looking for bird

droppings, you are sure to see weeds and plants at the foot of buildings, or between paving-stones, or in gutters. However good the street cleaning is, there are bound to be places where brushes can't easily reach. There will be mosses of various kinds, fresh and green after rain. You will also find chickweed and shepherd's purse, and possibly daisies, dandelions, groundsel, and sow thistles. A street flora would be interesting to compile. Occasionally very surprising plants are found. A paved yard has been known to produce hemp (hashish) because the owner cleaned birdcages there and sometimes hosed the yard, so that seeds were able to germinate.

Often a concrete path develops a crack, and it is interesting to see what happens there over a period. Before long there is dust, and soil, then odd plants, and if you scrape the soil away you will find insects such as springtails, leather jackets and wireworms. Other insects you will have to search for in towns include the *privet hawk moth*, the larvae of which feed on privet, so even dusty little front garden hedges are worth looking at, in spring and summer; the *buff ermine moth*, in virginia creeper, and the yellow *swallowtail moth* in ivy. A possible place for plants and insects is round the foot of trees planted in streets. These tend to be very dry dusty areas, overshadowed by the trees themselves and with impoverished soil. But even here sampling will reveal a soil fauna. In country towns you might also see there traces of squirrels, at the foot of the trees, but not if these are isolated as squirrels travel from tree to tree. Occasionally you may even find owl pellets, little grey balls of indigestible matter – fur, bones, skin – regurgitated. These can be analysed and the contents identified, so you know what the owl has been eating. Sometimes litter boxes are placed at the foot of trees, and in this case you may find evidence of mice and rats. Ice-cream cartons with sugary liquid left in them may attract insects.

Empty tins, sometimes filling with rain water and then getting hot in the sun, also provide a new type of habitat, although not a long-lasting one. Foxes have been known to search dustbins, but only in the suburbs.

Trees planted in streets tend to be of the small ornamental kind, such as almond and cherry. But if conditions allow, naturalists would prefer to have larger trees, preferably those you would find in a native British woodland, such as oak, ash and elm. These, especially oak, tend to support a much richer variety of insect life than the others. The oak tree has been found to provide a habitat for as many as 284 insect species. Avenues of lime, or horse chestnut, are splendid, where there is room for them. The lime trees of Berlin are famous, and the chestnut trees of Paris. Two non-native species often seen in Britain are the London plane, good in street conditions, and the robinia, or false acacia, noticeable for its fresh green foliage. Any of these can be studied as habitats, but the trees themselves are worth study – which trees do best where, how they respond to the seasons and weather, and in what manner the leaves appear and unfold. Aerial views of towns often show a much larger tree population than one would expect from the ground. Comparison of some towns with others, or parts of a town with other parts, could yield interesting results, especially if correlated with bird surveys.

Trees in town are sometimes affected by air pollution. Gases from the exhaust pipes of cars may make it difficult for them to thrive. Evergreens, particularly firs and pine trees, are sensitive also to sulphur dioxide, given off in smoke from chimneys. Garden plants in towns may show blotching of the leaves from this cause. Dust and soot on leaves is damaging. In some areas (admittedly the worst industrial areas) two pounds of dirt fall on a square yard of ground every year. A white handkerchief hung on a washing line is a simple but effective indicator of visible atmospheric pollution.

From every point of view, it is very desirable that air pollution should be reduced in towns. In December 1952, smog in London – that is, a combination of smoke and fog – is believed to have killed four thousand people. Another incident in 1957 killed many cattle at the Smithfield Show. If people and cows are killed, what effects may there be on other animals – domestic pets, and such forms of animal life as can exist in a city? Under the Clean Air Act, 1956, local councils can enforce smokeless zones, and where this has already been done, an enormous improvement has been brought about. If the air were cleaner, buildings would be free from the black coating so many of them now have. People, animals and vegetation could breathe more freely. Then if trees were planted wherever there is room – some big, some small, some specimen trees set round with flagstones or cobbles, some in small thickets of flowering shrubs, with daffodils and grass naturalized round them – *all* our cities could become garden cities.

CHURCHES AND CHURCHYARDS

Before we leave the street scene, there is another very special type of area there, of great interest for nature, although it is often neglected by naturalist and conservationist. This is the churches and churchyards of Britain. There are a great many of them – a city such as Norwich has more than thirty – and they are of exceptional importance because so many of them are right in the middle of built-up areas, where open space is so limited. Even in towns, most of our churchyards still possess magnificent trees. The evergreens are often particularly fine, especially the old yews, with their red and purple berries so beloved of thrushes and blackbirds. Holm oak is often found, and the Scots pine. To make these areas

82

ANIMALS AND PLANTS IN A
CHURCH YARD

1. LICHEN
2. YEW
3. HEDGEROW SNAIL
4. TAWNY OWL
5. LESSER HORSESHOE BAT
6. LONG-TAILED FIELD MOUSE

into bird sanctuaries would require only a few steps – such as planting more berrying shrubs, and others giving nesting places; leaving old trees and stumps; putting up bird boxes of different kinds, if old hollow trees are not available; planting thick hedges; providing water, and some winter feeding; creating a wild and undisturbed area for shelter and nesting. The Royal Society for the Protection of Birds has produced a leaflet suggesting methods of making school playgrounds into bird sanctuaries, but the quiet and age of churchyards make them even more suitable.

Even the gravestones are of great interest, especially when left standing and untouched. They provide a suitable place for the growth of lichens and mosses. In the built-up area of London, within a radius of Charing Cross, 165 species of lichen have been recorded (although only 71 have been seen since 1950). Most of them are on gravestones. The nitrogen they need for their growth seems to be supplied by birds which perch on the stones. These plants are of extraordinary interest, although their study is complicated and difficult. They are particularly useful today because they can act as indicator species for air pollution, being unable to grow in the areas of worst degradation, so that one biologist has said that in Britain we should aim at 'air fit for lichens and rivers fit for trout'.

Again, because churches are usually much the oldest buildings in the areas round them, their walls may be of special interest. Ferns growing in them may include harts tongue, spleenwort, and brittle bladder ferns, and there may be algae, mosses, and liverworts. Other plants include pellitory of the wall, and the fascinating, pretty little ivy-leaved toadflax. Indeed many flowering plants are found in walls, such as wall rocket, stonecrop, valerian, and wallflowers. The walls of Ludlow Castle have been described as hanging gardens full of snapdragons, wallflowers, greater celandine, feverfew, wall rocket, red valerian, marjoram, and harebell. A survey of old walls in Middlesex showed that over 211 different species of wild plants were growing on them. If rebuilding or re-pointing of old walls is necessary, perhaps efforts could be made to see that some specimens of all species found are allowed to remain. Interesting studies can be made of the adaptation of plants to living on walls, the effect of broken walls and weathering, the differences between sunny and shady walls, and the effect of different materials on plant life. On damp walls there will be snails and slugs – in September snails begin to hide away for the winter, and they seal themselves into their shells with their own slime. You can often find them in wall crevices. Lizards, and mammals such as mice, stoats, or weasels, may also make their homes in cracks and hollows.

There are also many grassy areas to be found in our churchyards. Just as in gardens, these are more valuable for wild life if the grass is slightly longer than usual. Then voles may live there – food for tawny and little owls – and butterflies, and bumble bees. Molehills will be less of a nuisance in rough grass, so that there need be no attempt to drive moles away. Moreover, areas of uncut grass can be reserves of plants and plant associations that are becoming increasingly rare. In many parts of England permanent pasture – grass left un-ploughed, and unweeded – is being almost eliminated. In America, a search is having to be made in old grave-yards for some of the native plants which have disap-peared from cultivated prairies, and are now needed again to rejuvenate the land. In our own chuchyards, perhaps an acceptable policy for parts of them would be to cut the grass twice a year, first after the spring flowering in June, and then once only before the winter, and at neither time too short. More closely-grown paths can be made, as the contrast between short and rough grass can be very effective.

Finally, what about bats? These too require old buildings with ledges, crevices, and odd corners, the older the better. Church towers are one of their main habitats. They are often not liked, and inside a church they can

FLOWER CALENDAR
MAKE A FLOWER CALENDAR FOR STREETS, WASTE GROUND, CAR PARKS, AND OTHER SITES IN THE TOWN. THESE ARE SOME OF THE FLOWERS YOU MAY FIND.

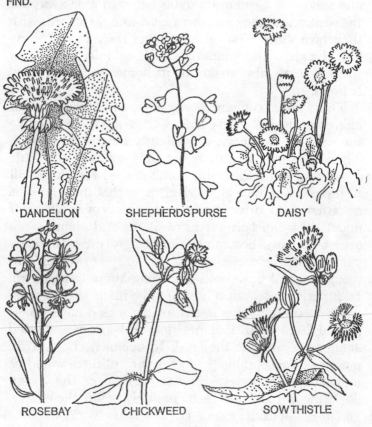

DANDELION   SHEPHERDS PURSE   DAISY

ROSEBAY   CHICKWEED   SOW THISTLE

cause dirt and damage. But if possible let us make a plea for them not to be destroyed. It would be a pity if they were all driven from their homes. It would be one more loss to chalk up in the history of disappearing species and vanishing animals.

8

IN THE PARK

MANY of the splendid urban and civic parks all over Britain are gardens rather than areas of countryside. Nature often has to take second place to gardening and recreation. Tennis courts, bowling greens, bandstands, playgrounds and paddling pools, are the conventional attractions. Moreover, in the past, gardeners made it their pride and joy to plant out large beds with ordinary annual flowering plants. A favourite scheme used to consist of red geraniums, white alyssum, and blue lobelia, to demonstrate patriotism. Many of these beds, together with formal rose gardens, flowering clocks, and memorial gardens, were triumphs of the gardener's art, but had little wild life interest. Fortunately, from the point of view of the naturalist, changes of fashion have led to much freer styles of gardening, with greater dependence on trees and shrubs, and shortages of labour have inevitably led to overgrown corners and wilder areas. For every kind of wild life – animals, birds, weeds, and insects – these are changes for the better. So today these parks offer unrivalled opportunities for close study of a limited range of wild life. It is true that familiarity with human beings has tamed some birds and beasts. The woods round Vienna, for instance, have large notices warning the visitor to beware of the wild boars. But in practice, as you enter the woods and leave your car, you are surrounded by grunting and extremely tame pigs begging for food. In the same way, the pelicans in St James's Park in London allow us to approach them much more closely than we ever could in their natural homes. So behaviour has been modified, in many cases.

THE GARDENS OF BUCKINGHAM PALACE

What then can we expect to find in these parks, situated as they often are in the very middle of towns? The gardens of Buckingham Palace have been more carefully studied than any other similar area. They are different from public parks, in that they are much less used, so that birds, for example, can breed in places and at heights where the nests would certainly be robbed elsewhere. On the other hand, the gardens have been entirely surrounded by high walls for over a hundred years. Outside the walls there is the biggest built-up area in the world, and pollution has been a serious factor, though less so now, since London's air became cleaner. Again, the gardens are so well cared for that there are few weeds, and no piles of leaf litter or old stumps, and so they lack many of the attractions so useful for nature in less tidy areas. But from the model studies made there by teams of specialist biologists, we can obtain clues as to the variety of wild life to be looked for in cultivated open spaces completely surrounded by streets and houses.

In the garden area of about 39 acres, scientists identified about 2,000 *taxa*, or forms of life. These included, in round figures:

> 600 different cultivated plants and trees
> 250 wild and naturalized plants and trees
> 33 mosses, liverworts and lichens
> 40 fungi

　　　　60 birds
　　　　 5 butterflies
　　　　34 moths
　　　　 2 mammals.

In addition to this list, there were many other insects, beetles, spiders, small invertebrate animals, and fish in the lake. From the list given, it follows that if your opportunities for observation are limited to public parks in towns, there would be a far greater variety of birds or moths than animals or butterflies for you to study. The only two mammals found were the mouse and the brown rat. A glimpse was obtained of one other small brown animal, probably a vole. This agrees with findings in other gardens and parks in built-up areas, but if the parks were situated on the outskirts of towns, instead of being islands of vegetation, there would certainly be squirrels, foxes, perhaps badgers, and moles.

The very small number of butterflies – red admiral, small tortoiseshell, small white, large white and holly blue – is largely due to the lack of the favoured food plants. The gardeners do their work so well that there are very few weeds of any size. Imagine so large a garden with not a single nettle in it anywhere. They have been completely wiped out. Newts, toads, and frogs are very scarce, and there are very few slugs and snails, again partly because the gardeners are far too tidy to leave debris lying about in which the animals can feed and breed.

The quiet and seclusion of the gardens permit a very varied bird life. About 20 kinds of birds actually nest and breed there. This compares with 17 in St James's Park (at the time the study was made; some of these numbers have increased since), 23 in Hyde Park, and 26 in Regent's Park – all of them very much larger than the Palace gardens. In addition to the breeding birds, others observed in the royal gardens included winter visitors, passage migrants, and occasional visitors such as the great spotted woodpecker, the magpie, and the cuckoo. So the bird watcher is not short of material, but it does seem that the number of breeding birds would be increased if there were more long grass, wildernesses, and overgrown shrubberies. Incidentally, there were no cats in the gardens.

The cultivated plants and trees of the Palace grounds are superb, and include many kinds of roses, camellias, rhododendrons, azaleas, lilies, delphiniums, and others. There are also many wild and naturalized flowers, even if weeds are ruthlessly eliminated. In recent years the number of wild plants recorded throughout central London is 475. At the Palace there were 260, and 50 of these were not found elsewhere in London. There are few plant associations, as would be found in the countryside, but there are in fact enough plants growing naturally to indicate what the vegetation would be if allowed to revert to a state of nature. Every year 'aliens' arrive, with bedding plants, shrubs, or in soil brought from outside, but they seldom survive. Strange plants from seed dropped near the bird table on the north terrace were soon rooted out. On the whole pollution does little harm today, even in gardens so closely hemmed in by a great city. Some of the evergreens drop their leaves in winter, unable to keep them in polluted conditions, but in fact most of them flourish. Altogether the limiting factors for nature and wild life at Buckingham Palace are lack of contact with the countryside, and the high standard of gardening.

LONDON PARKS

All the London parks are wonderful places for bird watching, and they are kept under very close observation, so that changes of all kinds – losses, new birds, new nesting sites – are carefully noted. Some of them have definite areas set aside as bird sanctuaries. According to the latest available surveys, the largest number per acre and the most varied list of species in the public parks are to be found in Regent's Park with the adjacent area of Primrose Hill. Over a hundred different kinds of birds are to be seen there, and more than a third of them breed successfully. Herons are frequent visitors, and the first known attempt of herons to nest in Inner London took place there in 1968. Buzzards, peregrines, sparrow hawks and kestrels have been observed; on one occasion 1,600 lapwings flew over during a two-hour watch; and infrequent visitors have been grey plover, snipe, greenshank, lesser black-backed gulls, collared doves, cuckoos, and little owls. Because of the changes made under the Clean Air Act, swifts and house martins have started to breed just outside the park, and swallows nesting in a shed in 1968 were the first to do so since 1908, when they nested at the Zoo. During 1968 on one solitary occasion a nightingale was seen.

The waterfowl collection on the lake in St James's Park is joined by many wild birds. Herring gulls, long-tailed ducks, great-crested grebes, teal, shovelers, and pochard are only some of the interesting birds to be seen there. Moorhen and coot nest in quite large numbers. The Highgate Ponds and the Kenwood Lake in north London are also notable for water birds – gadwall, shoveler, goldeneye and shelduck are sometimes there; kingfishers have been seen; and reed warblers are returning after long absences. The ornamental lakes in very many of our public parks are almost equally good places for bird study. Swans, mallard, and moorhens regularly nest in the larger parks with stretches of water.

These London and other parks are in many ways

Richmond Park

One might find these birds
in places marked.

Key

B   — Blackbird
H   — Heron.
MA — Mallard
O   — Owl
PW — Pied Wagtail
SW — Swan
W   — Wren

½ Mile

East Sheen Gate
Roehampton Gate
Pond
PW
MA
Beverley Brook
Golf Courses
B
QUEEN'S RIDE
CLOSED TO MOTOR TRAFFIC
Richmond Gate
Pond
W
B
O
PW
MA H
SW
MA
SW
H
Pond
B
Pond
Petersham Park
CLOSED TO MOTOR TRAFFIC
W
N
W
PW
CLOSED TO MOTOR TRAFFIC
Ham Gate
Robin Hood Gate
Kingston Hill
Kingston Gate

better and easier places for bird studies than the open fields and woodlands of our countryside, because space is comparatively limited, and the range of species is not so great as to be utterly confusing. Bird nesting habits could well be studied there – which birds choose which trees, the height of nests, the number of successful breeding birds, or the material used for nests. Another possibility is feeding habits – which birds eat which berries and fruits, and in what order. And there is still much to be learnt and recorded about bird song – the different times of the year during which the different birds can be heard, according to conditions such as temperature, wind, and rain, and also the total output of song of any one bird during the day. Some studies have been done on this last question. On one day in May a skylark was heard singing a total of 47 minutes out of a singing day of 13 hours 42 minutes. In July it sang 181 minutes out of a singing day of 17 hours 55 minutes. Making notes of this kind is a matter for great patience and accuracy, but you would learn a lot about birds doing it.

Most of the larger British mammals are both nocturnal and shy, so that parks are not the best places to look for them in, unless they are informal areas of woodland or open country, or situated next to such areas, with open access. In Richmond Park hares may be seen dancing in March, on the open ground. From time to time a fox may be glimpsed there. Squirrels are everywhere, and their dreys can be seen high in trees – most easily seen in winter, when the trees have lost their leaves. Weasels are also common. Rabbits have practically disappeared. In Richmond Park there are also two badger setts, each with a boar and sow, with their family. Badgers are actually more common than is often realized, but choose the least frequented places, so are often quite unobserved. There is a herd of fallow deer in Greenwich Park, and in Richmond Park as well as

94

fallow deer there are red or Scottish deer, ranging freely through the park.

Many species of fungi can be collected in parks. If you go on a fungus foray, you will need a large flattish basket, like a garden trug, to avoid crushing your specimens, and this is best lined with damp moss. Sheets of newspaper between layers will prevent damage. A few small tins may be useful, and a knife or trowel, in case some of the material on which the fungi are growing has to be cut away. Never take all the mushrooms or toadstools; one or two of each kind is enough, or if it is a large specimen, a piece of it will do, because what you are picking is the fruiting body, from which eventually new plants will be produced.

Spring is the time to find the cup fungi – a warm spring day after heavy rain should be productive. The most common of the cup fungi is the red elf cup, or pixie cup, one of the most attractive little fungi to be found. It is crimson red, round, and rather neat, curled up at the edges, having started as a hollow thin rubbery ball, opening out into a cup. It usually grows on dead branches, in damp mossy areas, or on bare soil. Another is the orange peel fungus, looking like bits of orange peel thrown down by the wayside. It is thinner than real orange peel, and is orange inside as well as out. If you take one home, and keep it in a saucer of damp moss in a sunny place, you may see faint clouds of orange spores rising from it. Look for it on newly-made paths, or where the earth has lately been disturbed.

In autumn other groups of fungi will be found, and again warm weather after rain is the best time. Often species of fungi are associated with particular trees. An example is the beef steak fungus, usually found on old oak trees. It is sometimes called the ox tongue, or poor man's beefsteak, being reddish brown in colour, its flesh looking and feeling like red meat. Similarly, the white butt rot is nearly always found on beech trees, where it causes serious and damaging heart rot. What has been called a 'give-and-take' relationship between certain fungi and the roots of certain trees often exists, apparently to their mutual advantage. In birch woods or near birch trees we often find the red flycap, or fly agaric, so called because its juice was at one time used as the poisoning agent in fly paper. The young white cap changes later to a brilliant scarlet, with white warts or patches. It is poisonous and dangerous, but not often fatal. It is this fungus which is used as the model in children's painting books, or for toys, or garden ornaments in association with plastic gnomes.

The jelly fungi include a number of oddities, and are found on trees, dead branches, or decayed wood. The best known is Jew's Ear, brownish flesh colour, ear-shaped, growing on elder. It is like jelly when moist, and goes bone-hard with age. Another well-known one is witches' butter, dark orange when dry, orange yellow when moist. It is contorted, and brain-like, in appearance, and is found on dead branches, hanging like a mass of jelly from the twigs.

Among the puffball kind of fungi are the true puffballs, earth balls, and stinkhorns. These are round, and hold the spores inside them; when they are ripe the spores are allowed to escape. The puffball opens with a hole at the top, and out of this puffs of brown smoke appear. The giant puffball is the largest fungus in Britain, and may be almost a foot across. The common earth ball is yellowish in colour, with cracks all over the upper surface, through which the spores escape; it may be rounded or bun-shaped. The stinkhorn makes use of flies to carry off its spores, and the first clue you will

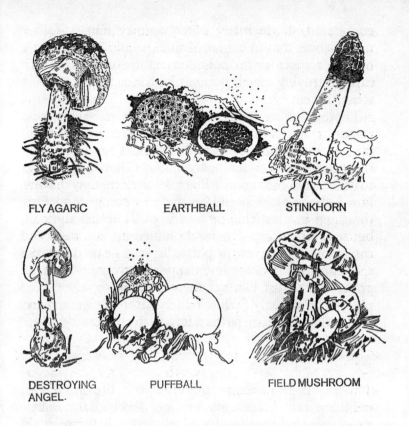

FLY AGARIC   EARTHBALL   STINKHORN

DESTROYING   PUFFBALL   FIELD MUSHROOM
ANGEL.

probably have as to its whereabouts is its smell, like rotten eggs.

How many of these fungi you will find in parks depends entirely on the local conditions. Look for them on trees, old stumps, and dead branches; also along the foot of hedges; by the side of paths; and on compost heaps. In grass you may see fairy rings, as they are called. These are made by fungi which grow outwards from the centre, leaving the middle dying, as they grow, so that every year they produce an ever-widening circle. The name shows how mysterious they have always been considered, as do many other country names. Other names show that in course of time people have learnt a healthy respect for the poisonous nature of fungi – death cap, destroying angel, poison pie, the sickener, are just some of them.

Photographing fungi where they are growing with a colour camera is a good idea, because it records the habitat and reproduces the right colours. They last a very short time if picked and taken home. Colours may begin to change almost at once. The inkhorn kind may dissolve into a sticky black liquid on the way home. Modelling the fungi in plasticine or wax is really rather difficult, but it can be done. The kind divided up into stem and cap – not the jellies or the puffballs – can be used to make spore prints. Try doing it with open mushrooms from the greengrocer. Just take off the cap of one of them, and place it on a sheet of white paper. After a few hours you will find an intricate pattern left on the paper.

A VARIETY OF LIFE

This is far from exhausting the wild life interest of public parks. In the gardens of Buckingham Palace there were 57 species of spiders, and this figure could well be exceeded in a large park outside an urban area. (The cellars of the Palace were examined, but they were too clean to give spiders much to eat and drink. One species was found which is confined to cellars and is imported with cases of French wine.) One of the team of scientists searched seven habitats for *Acari*, or terrestrial mites, including the carpet of moss under holly trees, humus near the lake, dry litter on bare ground under holly, litter under rose bushes, the manure heap, and long coarse grass. Others looked for harvestmen, centipedes and millipedes and woodlice. 26 species of worms were found. Snails and slugs, as has been said, were disappointingly scarce. Bristletails, springtails, (about 26 species), cockroaches, earwigs, mayflies, dragonflies, thrips, bugs, leaf-hoppers, scale insects and caddis flies were found. Beetles were there in large numbers, and the *Diptera* or flies included daddy-long-legs, winter gnats, mosquitoes, midges, horse flies, bluebottles, dung flies, and many others. The entomologist is never at a loss for material.

NATURE TRAILS IN PARKS

The difficulty in many parks is to know where to begin. For this reason, some of the local councils in Britain, who manage parks and gardens, while taking considerable trouble to enhance the wild life interest of these areas, have also set up nature trails, to give an idea of what to look for at different times of year. In Glasgow, the Parks Department has done this at Linn Park, with great success, because the park has many natural assets, a river running through it, different kinds of woods, a castle at one end, and an open golf course near by. The nature trail takes about three hours to walk round, and there are fifteen marked points at which to stop and look. The starting point, leading to the first post, and the post itself, give the chance of approaching and then entering a pine wood. In spring there are many wild flowers, such as bluebells, primroses, celandines, and wood sorrel. Wood pigeons will be nesting there, and inside the wood there may be traces of rabbits, birds' feathers, and owl pellets. A little later in the year, in paths by the wood, there will be germander speedwell, lady's smock, comfrey, wild violets, creeping-jenny, or wild strawberries, and in the pine woods there will be toadstools such as the fly agaric already mentioned, or another known as the shaggy parasol. In autumn these will be followed by fairy-rings. As the trees do not shed their leaves in autumn, many birds and small animals find shelter there. In winter the shapes of other trees can be studied. In some places a look out can be kept for kingfishers, tree creepers, swallows, larks, woodpeckers and owls, as well as all sorts of insects and plants. The visitor is given many suggestions on where to look for everything. In another Glasgow Park, Kelvingrove, there is also a nature trail, with 14 observation posts. The Parks Department has produced a useful illustrated guide book to this trail. They suggest that at one post you can mark out a square yard on the grass, and note down *everything* you find in it. Hints are given for identifiying the grasses, insects, tiny soil animals, and seeds, you might discover.

Some public parks are rather different because they have been formed out of the gardens and grounds of mansions or large houses, acquired for the purpose by local councils. Calderstones Park, in Liverpool, used to be a private estate. It gets its name from the calder stones, large stones thought to have been part of an ancient burial mound outside the park. The word 'calder' may come from 'gaulder', an Anglo-Saxon word meaning wizard or enchanter. The nature trail constructed in this park takes you round several interesting features, such as the 'ha ha', a sunken ditch with a stone retaining wall, built to keep cows straying into the gardens from fields beyond the park. Another feature deriving from its history as a family home is a large isolated mulberry tree, known as the fertility tree, as it was planted in the belief that while it survived there would be no break in the family line of inheritance.

A similar park with the same sort of history, and with a nature trail in it, is Witton Park, in Blackburn, which also belonged to a local family before it became a park in 1946. The ruins of the old house are still there, and have been colonized by a large variety of plants – gorse, broom, harebells, heather, and many others – trying to

Monks Wood Nature Trail

Key

1: Hotel Ride, one of the main entries to the wood.

2: Badger Ride, so-called because there used to be a badger sett at the far end.

3: Silver Birches, oaks, and wild privet.

4: Badger Ride Pond, once used for watering cattle or sheep, or perhaps a water supply for a human settlement.

5: Leeds Ride, named after an entomologist who worked in Monks Wood fifty years ago.

6: Barrow Ride, named after a burial mound or barrow used in pre-Roman days.

7: Neaverson's Ride, named after the man who owned the wood before it became a national nature reserve.

8: The Glade, an open area filled with interesting plants.

9: Aspens and silver birches.

10: Hotel Ride, leading back to Monks Wood Experimental Station.

11: An oak tree with a hole in the trunk made by a great spotted woodpecker.

———— Reserve Boundary

•••••• Stopping Point

•••••• Rides

===== Paths

Monks Wood Experimental Station

Start

¼ Mile

establish themselves there. Trees introduced when it was still a private garden include an Atlantic cedar, a tree found in the Atlas Mountains of North Africa, and a monkey puzzle tree.

These are just a few examples of nature trails in parks, and as more local councils adopt the same policy of providing them public parks will become increasingly interesting to visit. If the park in your own town does not yet contain such a trail, you can make one for yourself – on paper, that is. To do this you will need to acquire a map of the park, or make your own by surveying it or make a diagram, on a large scale. Then you can mark on it anything of interest – special trees, a pond with water birds, places where you see butterflies – and think out a circular tour round these places, marking it on your map. If you made plans, maps, sketches, and took slides or snaps, and collected pictures from local newspapers, you could build up your material into a small exhibition. Or you could make it into a lecture, with a tape recording of your own voice pointing out things worth noticing. Then you might be able to raise a little money for local charities or nature conservation in your own area, by showing what you have done. But this is rather ambitious, and perhaps you would rather consider something easier. In that case, to give just one suggestion, having made your map of the park you could use it for bird surveys. You simply put down on the map an initial or a code whenever you see or hear a particular bird in a particular place – such as B for blackbird, or R for robin. Then you can mark by strokes after the initial the number of times you see that bird in the same place – e.g. B///(Blackbird, three times), R//////// (Robin, eight times) and so on. You may find some birds are fairly constant to the same patch of ground, such as individual robins dividing up the park between them, while others, for instance the wood pigeon, fly about all over the place. As you get more familiar with different birds you can add to the list, but you must miss out sparrows, because there are too many of them, and perhaps starlings as well.

9

DUMPS AND DERELICTION

MAN-MADE habitats vary enormously in type and interest. They include derelict building sites, gasworks, markets, river banks, car parks, and road verges. Marshalling yards and docks are rather different. Best of all, from the variety of wild life to be found there, are dumps and sewage works, and best for birds are waterworks and reservoirs near towns. Once permission to study in these areas has been obtained, the way is clear for absorbing and valuable work.

DERELICT SITES AND WASTE GROUND

Plants and seeds reach derelict areas in strange ways. Nearly a hundred years ago a survey was made by a botanist of five waste sites in London, all of them in or near the city. Seventy-eight species of plants were found, and thirty-four of them – the biggest single group – were thought to have been distributed from horses' nosebags. Seeds were dropped from them and then grasses and cereals developed. The wind brought many other seeds, such as willow herbs, coltsfoot, dandelion, groundsel, ragwort, sow thistles, and fleabane. The seeds of five common weeds were brought by birds – shepherd's purse, swine's cress, mouse-eared chickweed, common chickweed, and knotgrass. And then there were twenty-four plants apparently escapes from flower gardens or vegetable plots, ranging from opium poppies to cabbages.

Widespread interest in derelict sites was aroused during the Second World War, by the spectacular invasion of London's bombed sites by plants and animals. Within a year of the first German bombs on the city, some of the devastated areas had turned almost into gardens, and by 1952 the list of wild flowers, grasses and ferns had risen to 269 varieties. It has been said that the Irishman's dream of London as paved with silver and gold came true, for the bombed sites were covered with silver (Canadian fleabane) and gold (Oxford ragwort).

First of the plants to appear were algae, mosses and ferns, because the spores of these plants are always in the air, ready to colonize whenever an opportunity occurs. The wind brought many light seeds, especially those of the colourful rosebay willow herb. Sandbags brought for defence purposes contained the seeds of grasses and even seaside plants. Horses' fodder still contributed some kinds, but more came from discarded bird seed and pet food. Office workers in the city started having their sandwich lunches on these sites, as they grew attractive, and so an odd assortment of edible plants began to grow, from apples, tomatoes, plums, dates, cherries, and even figs. Many of these lunch-time visitors scattered packets of garden seeds over the areas. Generally it is a mistake to do this, as alien seed in wild areas may thrive at the expense of other native plants and may even become run-away invaders. But on the London sites they did no harm. Stranger seeds were brought by passing cars. Some species from America seem to have come on the tracks and tyres of military vehicles and tanks. Butterflies and moths soon followed the plants. The caterpillars of the red and black cinnabar moth fed on

the leaves of ragwort, and those of the elephant
hawkmoth on rosebay willow herb. Rats, mice, cats and
stray dogs were numerous, and other animals included
hedgehogs, tortoises, lizards, snakes, and lost or discarded pets. It was at this time that the black redstart
became noticed as a breeding species in London. A well-
known garden shrub, the buddleia, only introduced into
this country less than a hundred years ago, became a
very common sight on derelict areas.

Today building sites may be less rich in flora and
fauna because they are not usually left undisturbed for
long periods. But there are some new factors that make
investigations into waste land just as interesting. It is
known that trains carry seeds from one area to another –
the Oxford ragwort appears to have been spread in this
way – but what is not certain is how the replacement of
steam trains by electrically driven ones will affect the
plant life of railway embankments. Hot ash thrown on
to the embankments, in the days of steam, burnt off
much of the scrub and allowed flowers such as primroses
and cowslips to thrive. Nowadays this may not be the
case. Nor do we know just how important is traffic as a
method of seed dispersal. In June 1968, an investigator
tried to test this. He used a car the tyres of which had
been scrubbed clean, and then drove it 65 miles after
heavy rain along roads in the South Midlands, and
finally hosed it down and collected the sediment from
the wash. Then he used sterilized horticultural compost
to see what would grow. He obtained seedlings from 13
different flowering plants, including 387 seedlings
of annual meadow grass, 274 of chickweed, and 220 of
rayless mayweed or pineapple weed. Ships are well
known to carry cargoes of unexpected seeds and insects.
What about aeroplanes? Will they bring plant stowa-
ways? It seems we are unlikely to take or get accidental
plants from the moon, but if space ships ever visit Mars

ANIMALS AND PLANTS ON REFUSE TIPS

1. CREEPING THISTLE
2. ABANDONED PET DOG
3. STARLING
4. BLACK-HEADED GULL
5. BROWN RAT

or any planet where there may be life, strict precautions will have to be taken, in both directions. All this needs watching.

NEW HOMES FOR WILD LIFE

Rubbish tips are extraordinarily interesting as a habitat for wild life. Grapes, melons, tomatoes – these plants were found growing on a tip near London fifty years ago. In a survey of five of the biggest London tips, two hundred and fifty different plants were found. Many of them were native British species, but 170 of them were aliens, brought from all sorts of places. There was a forest eight feet tall of giant hogweed and great docks. There were many different cereals, probably from chicken food, and garden flowers such as delphiniums, hollyhocks, mignonette, and night-scented stock. Escapes from vegetable gardens then included lettuce, beetroot, spinach, and artichokes. There were surprising plants from Africa and India. This was many years ago, but more recently very detailed work has been done on rubbish tips in many parts of the country. This shows that although conditions vary enormously, as there are different methods of dealing with the material brought, and the refuse itself varies so much, many forms of life can be studied on tips, whether you are interested in algae and mosses, fungi, British native plants, alien plants, insects, birds, or soil animals. There is more diversity on a refuse tip than on any other area of the same size anywhere in the country.

Apart from the interest of finding and identifying various forms of life, these refuse dumps give opportunities for working on many interesting ideas. As an example, we can take the question of plant dispersal and establishment. The succession of plants on a dump is interesting – the first plants to colonize, the changing conditions and how they affect subsequent plant life, and the final result. The ways in which plants exploit themselves to adapt to what are really very artificial conditions of life for them are fascinating. In any other form of life we should consider them very clever. For instance, creeping thistle is a troublesome weed, in many areas, especially in ploughed land. But the roots of the thistle are of such a kind that they really like being cut up and dispersed, so that ploughing, and other hard work intended to get rid of weeds, actually increases their possibilities of survival and increase. This might happen on rubbish tips – the more disturbance on the tips, and the more the plant roots are chopped up, the more plants you would get. Similarly, couch grass spreads by rhizomes bearing buds at the nodes, so that breaking up these slender parts leads to more, not fewer, plants. The more effort you put into trying to get rid of them, the more likely it would be that they were able to spread. An even better example of what one would like to call applied intelligence is seen in the common weed known as fat hen, or goosefoot. It is an annual plant, and produces many seeds. But these seeds are not all alike in their behaviour. Some of them germinate immediately after harvesting – that is, they do not show dormancy. But other seeds from the same plant do show dormancy. They may lie buried, and then when disturbed they may react to the cold; they may germinate in response to the cold. Some of the seeds are brown, some black; some smooth, some reticulated, and they may all have different times and conditions for their germination. In this way fat hen is sure to go on living, as a species, because it is not restricted to one set of conditions before it can reproduce itself. Few animals (except man) can do this. It is as if a jungle animal, such as a lion, could produce twins, one able to thrive in the tropics, and the other in the Arctic.

Visits to refuse dumps would be very useful if you intended to become a *chiropterist* – that is, a student of bats. Your first reaction might be to go to church, to find your bats; but in practice a refuse dump might provide better chances of your seeing them. Insects are plentiful there, because of the refuse and garbage, and these insects in their turn will attract bats. The *pipistrelle* bat is by far the most common species in Britain, but other kinds found on dumps include the *noctule* (common in southern England and Wales, less so further north, and nowhere common in Scotland), the *serotine*, also mainly in parts of southern England, *Daubenton's bat*, fairly common everywhere, and *Leisler's bat*, locally common throughout Britain. Brown rats are everywhere and will eat amost anything. Mice may also be very numerous. On one site of seven acres in Essex, it was thought that the population of mice was about 30 in winter and between 700 and a thousand in autumn. Lizards may also be found, sunning themselves on warm surfaces, as well as frogs and newts, and natterjack toads may be more frequent than has been realized. Regrettably, abandoned pet dogs often appear on tips, famished and neglected, as they do round litter bins on motorways.

The effect of tips on bird life has been to provide many of them with a new and favourable habitat. It seems that certain species need open surroundings in which to establish breeding territories, and in default of more ordinary sites some of them have moved on or near to tips. Examples given are wheatear, whinchat, skylark, tree-pipit, corn-bunting, and reed-bunting. Insects will attract other birds, weeds and plant garbage still others. Scavenging birds include all members of the crow family, including rooks, jackdaws, and carrion crows. Starlings are nearly always present in hundreds if not thousands, and the availability of food on the refuse tips appears to have had a marked effect on both the numbers and the behaviour of gulls. The great black-backed gull, at one time almost entirely a maritime bird, now is a regular winter visitor inland, and both the black-headed gull and the herring gull have greatly increased in numbers. The common gull also appears in large numbers, especially in passage between February and April in parts of eastern England. These four species are nearly always present on the larger dumps in the east and south. The remarkable feature of their presence is not so much their numbers as the immense journeys they make every day from their distant evening roosts on the north London reservoirs or on the coast of east and southern England, to refuse dumps as far away as Cambridge and Bishop's Stortford. In other parts of England they make similar journeys.

On the whole it is probably true that the refuse dumps regularly attract large numbers of fairly common birds, but the rarities and the shyer birds with more specialized requirements are not usually to be found on them. This is not true of that other great artificial man-made habitat, the inland waters and especially the reservoirs near London (elsewhere in the country to a lesser extent), and also sewage farms and gravel pits. The pick of the year for Londoners would certainly include visits to some of these areas. Man is often thought of as the great enemy of wild life. It is true he is busily destroying many natural habitats, but his activities are not all damaging. When he destroys homes for wild life he often creates new ones.

10

NIGHTSHIFT IN THE COUNTRY

IN Britain today it is easier to see a lion than a hare, an elephant than a badger. It is true you would have to go to a zoo, to see lions and elephants; but once there, you would be almost certain to find them, whereas you might spend lots of time in the country without ever seeing hares, badgers, or any of the animals of the countryside. Many people who live all their lives in the country have never set eyes on such creatures as badgers or otters. All our native British animals are both shy, and largely nocturnal, so that you have to know where to begin looking for them, and it helps to know a few tricks of the trade.

HOW TO SEE WILD LIFE

One of these tricks of the trade is to look first for the characteristic traces of the animal, rather than the animal itself. Tracks can easily be seen in snow, and sometimes in soft mud by streams. Some animals, such as deer, badgers, and rabbits, tend to follow already existing trackways, whereas cats and foxes are more individualistic, avoid existing trails and making their own way along hedges and across fields. Some try to keep to cover, such as hedgerows, ditches, and river banks – stoats, weasels, rats and water voles do this. You can

NOT LIFE SIZE

DOG

DOMESTIC CAT

STOAT

BROWN HARE

OTTER

HEDGEHOG

ROE DEER

BROWN BAT

BADGER

FOX

soon learn to recognize their footprints. And once having spotted these prints, you then know where to look for the animals, because many of them do not stray very far, and may return time after time to the same places. The fox, for instance, may patrol regularly at set times round his own domain. Another way of tracing animals to their haunts is to look for their droppings, or scats, again very characteristic.

Even easier to spot are mole hills. They are very often found in groups in the corners of fields, or by hedges; you can often see them from the train, as you rush through the countryside. When you have found them, examine the earth in them, to see whether it is fresh and moist. If so, you know at least one mole is working there. You may not be lucky enough to see him, but you can often see earth being thrown up, as the mole tunnels underneath the earth. Both during the day and the night the mole does very often emerge. Proof of this is the fact that moles are sometimes eaten by herons, and their remains are often found in the stomach contents of owls. The most likely time to see them above ground is June, when young moles are searching for homes and perhaps preparing to make tunnels.

Another trick of the trade is to go out in the early evening. Dusk is a time of intense activity in the world of nature. Strangely enough, your best chance of seeing a barn owl is in the beam of car headlights. He will come swooping down, looking white and ghostly, as he starts his nightly hunting. Owls of different kinds may be heard at any time of year, in any part of Britain, but numbers are falling, and each bird has a very large territory. Once you have seen an owl in a certain place, you know where to continue looking. You may hear him calling all night. Most of the time he is simply stating who he is. If you hear another owl apparently replying to him, they are not exactly carrying on a conversation.

They are telling each other to keep to their own patches. Do you think you would like an owl picnic? With plenty of warm clothes, and flasks full of hot drinks, you could stay up all night in a place where you have already heard an owl (perhaps a wood or a churchyard) and mark down all through the night the exact times you heard the owl call.

Another animal often seen in the beam of car headlights is the hare. He seems to be dazzled or hypnotized by the lights, and will run ahead of you for miles, if you drive slowly behind him. But there are more hares about than owls, and they are not so difficult to find by day although dusk is a good time to see them. If you sit quietly in the corner of a field alongside a road where you have already noticed one, you are very likely to see him again either in the day or the evening. It is said hares are very inquisitive, so that if you do something peculiar, he is bound to come along to investigate. One suggestion is that you should sit in the field with your legs up in the air. The hare will be so puzzled he will be irresistibly drawn to come along to see what is happening – or so it is said. You will be very lucky if you see hares at their maddest, in March. Their odd behaviour then has not been fully explained. Country people sometimes see two of them standing up, apparently boxing, and this may be part of the courtship ritual. Once a hare was seen on her hind legs punching a bullock on the nose, perhaps to protect her young.

At dusk too starling are at their noisiest, and country roosts are even bigger than those in towns. Some of them hold over a million birds. Day after day they follow the same flight paths, arriving in the same places at the same time, and taking a long time to settle down, as they talk or argue all at once. Rooks also roost in great crowds, gathering together in huge numbers in autumn and winter, before converging in what have been called 'super-roosts'. In winter, before darkness comes, birds visit the garden bird table for a final meal. Robin is usually last to leave, but wrens are also late going to bed. Pheasants may cluck about nearly all night. At almost any time of year many birds like to give a final burst of song, before settling down. Even in February, astonishing full song may be heard. In warmer weather, say in summer, flycatchers will be seen hovering round the garden, especially over compost heaps, catching insects on the wing. Swifts will be taking off, flying out to sea, sleeping as they fly. As other birds quieten down for the night, the song of the nightingale may be heard. The birds do sing during the day, as well as at night, but it is often difficult to hear them then, with so much other sound going on. Having spent the winter in the African tropics, the male birds arrive about ten days before the females and then compete to attract them, perhaps using song to do so. Kent and East Anglia are places to hear them. Warm still nights in late April and May are best, and although gardens, parks and commons are frequented, a quiet woodland is the most likely place to hear them. Again it is true that once you have found them you are likely to find them there regularly, night after night, and year after year, although sometimes for quite unknown reasons a pair will leave a familiar and long-used site. The nests are well hidden, in thick undergrowth, often on or close to the ground, in thickets or rough patches of shrubby woodland. As agriculture becomes so efficient in using every square inch of land suitable nesting sites are disappearing. The birds are difficult to see. They keep well away from people, but they may have favourite trees in gardens.

Butterflies disappear long before dark, even on warm summer evenings. The flowers of the day close their petals, but others open and give out fragrance. Night-scented stock, tobacco flowers, evening primroses, valerian, and phlox will all be visited by moths. If you take a lantern outside you will see them dancing; it is their time for flying, feeding, and mating. Most of the Noctuid moths are active only at night. To study them you can paint a sweet sticky liquid on a tree or wooden fence, and then watch them come. A mixture of brown sugar, beer, and rum, used to be recommended, but honey or treacle will do. Put a vertical streak downwards from about eye level, and do it just as the daylight is beginning to fade. Open rides or clearings in woodlands are good places. The moths will come to feed and you can watch them at close quarters with a torch.

HEDGEHOGS ARE ODD

While you are watching moths, you are very likely to hear a hedgehog, again at dusk on warm summer evenings. Almost everything written and said about hedgehogs needs to be tested. There is still much we don't know about this very odd and eccentric animal. We don't even know how many there are – estimates have varied from one to twenty-five per acre – and we don't know whether their numbers are falling or not. Here is a fascinating field of study for the amateur naturalist, especially because hedgehogs are not at all predictable in their behaviour, and can often be seen and heard doing peculiar things at peculiar times.

The best places to find them are dry ditches in fields, parks or gardens, or among coarse grass at the foot of hedges, or in patches of rough grass, often in thick tussocks. They are most active between dusk and about 2 or 2.30 a.m., and from April to October, although these times and dates are very variable. They don't emerge far from their sleeping places in wet weather, and on dry summer evenings they may wait for the dew to bring out the insects and small animals on which they feed. If you

HEDGEHOG

stand quietly by a rough hedge, or walk slowly along with frequent pauses, you may very well hear one rustling through the grass. He may make considerable noise, crashing through leaves, rubbing against bark, and snorting or hissing. Once you know where abouts he lives, you will be able to find him again, as each one stays fairly close to his home area, not usually moving more than a hundred yards away. With a small portable tape recorder it is possible to take down the noise of his travelling, and also his grunts and snorts. Other noises are high-pitched whistles, evidently a form of communication between mother and young, and occasionally perfectly dreadful screams. You may also hear him crunching worms!

Courtship and mating look like a fight between two animals, with both of them pivoting, circling round, and snorting. This has been seen any time from April to September, most usually in May. The young are born after about thirty days, in litters of two to nine, five being usual. At first the mother feeds them herself, and later takes them out for walks, foraging, in line. If a nest is disturbed she may carry them one by one to another. After a month or so they look after themselves. Hedgehogs are fairly easily tamed, and can be induced to unroll by stroking or (it is said) by pouring water over them. Someone once did it with beer and is said to have turned his pet into a lifelong alcoholic. They will come regularly each evening if bread and milk are put out for them, but if they find the dish empty they may throw it about in a tantrum. Several of them may establish a peck order, they may disagree, or they may feed amicably all together. They may have fights with a scrubbing brush, or they may cuddle it. Favourite foods in captivity may include baked beans, mincemeat, cake and puffed wheat; sweet tea or coffee may be liked, and there are stories of them eating chocolate creams, ginger nuts, and blancmange. They can climb, run, and swim, but some of them either can't or won't. They are said to steal eggs, drink milk oozing from a cow's udder, or impale apples on their spines – but you will be lucky if you actually see them doing any of these things. They seem to suffer occasionally from madness or brain damage, and can then be seen running round in frantic circles, always anti-clockwise. Wayward, mysterious, and often bad-tempered creatures.

BADGERS ARE SHY

Much more difficult to study, but even more fascinating, are badgers, also creatures of the night. They are intensely suspicious wary animals. Hedgehogs often take very little notice of your presence, and do not object to being studied by torchlight; but badgers will be off and away at the slightest sound or smell of a human being. Occasionally you may see one in the daytime; if you are wandering quietly in undisturbed woodland then you may get a glimpse of one enjoying the sunshine or on his way to his latrine. Otherwise you must look for him in the night-time, again on warm evenings, best of all in June or July, and even then you will not see him unless you have previously located his home.

This is most likely to be in hilly woodland country – a wooded bank of soft soil, neither too crumbly nor too heavy for the animal to work, well above a stream or ditch, with old trees and some undergrowth, but not too far from some open space – this is where to look. Here the badger may make his sett, sometimes called a badger 'town', or earth. These may be found almost in any county of Britain, but in East Anglia and Scotland, and some other areas, they are rare. In Cornwall more than a hundred earths have been located. Elsewhere they may be more frequent than is generally known, being often in remote woodland. Farmers and gamekeepers often know where they are, and as many of them are situated on landed estates, their owners too are often aware of them. There may be several setts fairly close together, and some of them may be hundreds of years old. Often several different families use the same setts, or visit each other in their homes.

On the ground, one may see several large holes, sometimes under the roots of trees. There may be four, five, six or more entrances, but it seems that one of them will be the main door, more constantly in use than the others. Underground these entrances lead to an astonishing series of passages and rooms, from which great piles of earth have been excavated. Dry bedding is regularly taken into the earths, and damp or dirty bedding removed. These piles of dry ferns and grass often have a faint musty smell, typical of the badger. From the doors lead paths in different directions, often well worn, and indeed often used as paths by human beings, although from time to time they may disappear underneath a tree or some other obstacle the human has to skirt. These paths lead to other entrances, or to drinking water, or to the latrines used by all the animals. These consist of a series of small pits dug in the ground. As each is filled fresh ones are started.

The animals are extremely engaging to watch, if you are able to do this. Again, a warm summer evening; dusk; take up your position against a tree, or preferably up in it, if you can be comfortable there for hours at a time; and wait. A cautious sniffing may be heard; the boar may raise his head, beautifully striped in black and white; when he is satisfied everything is safe, he will emerge and start scratching himself. A few minutes later the sow may follow, and then the cubs; but the slightest suspicion will send them back into the ground. The boar may move off to the latrine, while mother and young play. Later, if all is safe, they will go off hunting; it is impossible to follow them, as they hear the slightest sound. If a large sett is being watched, it is essential to have a sentinel at each hole, to see how many animals emerge, and what times they return. Before they finally retreat, the young ones will certainly have a game – king of the castle, tag, or some other recognizable romp. They even have regular playgrounds! They spend much time scratching, and cleaning themselves. The mother trains her offspring diligently, and regularly 'combs' them for fleas and other parasites. Food is both meat and vegetable; moles, rats, beetles, and worms may be taken; rarely, a lamb or chickens.

So far, on a warm night, you may have been able to tape record hedgehogs, and photograph badgers. As dawn draws near, you will need the tape recorder again. All through the night there are strange sounds – rustlings, foxes barking (more frequently in the early part of the year, when they find their mates), owls hooting, and bats twittering, if you can hear them. Just before dawn, as it is growing light, the dawn chorus of birds begins. It is this you may wish to record.

Before doing so, you need to know the various songs of different birds, to be able to sort them out, and you need to get into position very early. By 4 o'clock, or even earlier (Greenwich Mean Time) birds are moving about, stretching, getting ready for the day; and then they sing. Late April, or early May, is the time. What you will hear depends completely on the area where you live, and what part of the country it is. The following times were once recorded by a woodland edge in Bedfordshire, in April.

4.15 a.m.	Nightingale
	Woodcock
	Skylark
	Cock Pheasant
	Crow
	French or red-legged Partridge
	Song Thrush
	Magpie
4.20 a.m.	Grasshopper Warbler
	Cuckoo
	Little Owl
	Tawny Owl
	Lady Amhurst's Pheasant
	Whitethroat
	Wood Pigeon

4.35 a.m.	Blackbird
4.40 a.m.	Hedge Sparrow
4.45 a.m.	Yellowhammer
4.50 a.m.	Wren
4.58 a.m.	Coal Tit
5.2 a.m.	Black Cap
5.15 a.m.	Nuthatch
	Gold Crest

The list might be quite different elsewhere, but it is always worth getting up early for. Once you feel sure you can identify the song of so many different birds, you might arrange with a friend in a different part of the country to get up early one morning when you can also do it, and both take notes of what you hear. You would both have to jot down weather conditions – wet or dry, windy or still, and temperatures – and then compare notes.

If you *can* ever borrow a small portable tape machine, as suggested, you will find it a fascinating business, making recordings of wild life. It's more difficult than one might think, to get good recordings, but it is particularly useful for bird song, because having once got your recording you can get an expert to help you identify the birds – this is why it is a good idea to try to record the dawn chorus.

11

WHO'S WHO IN CONSERVATION

AS soon as you start reading about conservation, or listening to other people, you find yourself brought up short by a confusing array of initials. The R.S.P.B., the S.P.N.R., B.B.O.N.T., S.S.S.I. – these are only a few of them. Behind these initials stands a complicated network of organizations and societies playing a great part in protecting nature in Britain, and many of them have a great deal to offer to the young naturalist.

THE NATURE CONSERVANCY

Starting with Government agencies, and trying to avoid initials, the body chiefly responsible for nature conservation in Britain is the *Nature Conservancy*. The Conservancy's headquarters are in London, and it has regional offices covering England, Scotland, and Wales, plus a number of research stations. It co-operates with many other organizations, both in Britain and in Europe, to promote the cause of conservation, but its most important function is to carry out research into the various problems of conservation (to be able to advise the Government on what should be done) and to manage the national nature reserves which have been set up. Much of the research work is highly specialized, undertaken by teams of scientific workers, but in some of it the co-operation of naturalists is very welcome. An example is the work of the *Biological Records Centre*, which co-ordinates the survey work of individuals and societies throughout the country, to make complete and continuous records of what forms of life exist in Britain, where they are, their numbers, and the changes occurring in our countryside. Another example on a smaller scale is the *Hedgerow Survey*, part of an extraordinarily interesting inquiry into the value of hedges for wild life and the possible results of their removal in large areas of the country. The organizers of the survey need much more detailed and complete information about hedges all over the country, and have issued a form of record to be filled up with information on how to do it.

NATURE RESERVES

The nature reserves managed by the Conservancy – now about 130 in number – have been described as living museums and outdoor laboratories, because of the important research work done there. The reserves are not chosen at random, nor are they simply places where rare plants or animals may be found. In the main, they are representative 'ecosystems'. Plants and animals do not occur in certain places by accident. They form part of characteristic associations, largely dependent on the underlying soil conditions. For instance, the Monks Wood National Nature Reserve, which is adjacent to one of the larger research stations of the Conservancy, is partly composed of oak and ash forest, with its accompanying flora and fauna. It is a surviving fragment of the great forests which used to cover the heavy clay plateau of Huntingdonshire. As such, it is the best remaining example of this kind of woodland, and supports an extremely interesting insect population. Another reserve, Saltfleetby-Theddlethorpe, in Lincolnshire, is quite different, covering sand dunes, saltings, and fresh-water marshes, each with typical plants and extremely interesting birds. The freshwater marsh includes such plants as sea rush, pond sedge, great water dock, and fen rush; smaller plants such as pennywort, marsh bed-straw, marsh arrow-grass, and skull-cap; and less common species such as bog pimpernel, water parsnip, brooklime, lesser water plantain and two different kinds of marsh orchid. It is also noteworthy as being the only Lincolnshire home of the natterjack toad. A third nature reserve which is different again is Widdybank Fell, in Upper Teesdale, where the underlying rock structure of shale, limestone, sandstone, and whin sill – described as a sandwich cake of rock – has produced a fascinatingly wide range of habitats, each with its quota of typical and often very localized plants. You might go to Monks Wood to listen to the nightingale; to Saltfleetby to see the shelduck; and on Widdybank Fell you would hear the curlew.

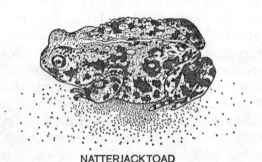

NATTERJACK TOAD

Because the reserves are primarily for research and conservation, they are not generally open to the public, and strict conditions have to be observed – no picking of flowers, no collecting, except under supervision. They are places where nature has to be protected and guarded. The Guide at Widdybank Fell includes a cry from the heart – *'Please take nothing but photographs!'* But in most of the reserves visits can be arranged, and in some of them nature trails have been planned to pinpoint the features of interest. At Holme Fen, in East Anglia, to give just one example, a trail of this kind has been laid out, and a printed guide is available. This reserve is on the deep black soil of the fen peat, and survives to show what the primeval fenland looked like. In addition to the national nature reserves, the Nature Conservancy also picks out sites of special scientific interest (S.S.S.I.s) which it notifies to the local planning authority, so that the needs of these areas can be borne in mind when development is contemplated.

THE FORESTRY COMMISSION AND THE COUNTRYSIDE COMMISSION

A second Government agency, very different from the Nature Conservancy but one of great importance in our countryside, is the *Forestry Commission*. Started originally as a commercial proposition to produce timber as part of the national economy, the Commission now holds nearly three million acres of land, two thirds of which are covered with forests and trees, and it has made much of this area available for public access and recreation. There are more than 140 car parks, forest trails, forest walks, information centres and camping sites. Probably the best known is the New Forest, in Hampshire, with its wild ponies, and deer, and its forest trail. Another well-known one is Thetford Chase, in

Norfolk, a vast expanse of pinewoods. Others range from historic forest such as Rockingham, in Northamptonshire, part of an old Crown Forest, and Savernake, in Wiltshire, also part of a historic forest, to areas of new mixed planting. Conservation and the preservation of wild life are much more part of the Commission's present policy than formerly, but are not its primary purpose. This is true also of a third Government agency, the *Countryside Commission*. This is responsible for national parks and areas of outstanding natural beauty. The Commission does not own these areas, but development in them including changes of land use is more strictly controlled than elsewhere, and the Commission maintains Information Centres to explain what facilities exist for walkers, campers, climbers and picnickers. It is also helping to organize the long-distance footpaths and bridleways such as the Pennine Way, a walk of 250 miles along the backbone of England. Beyond these three agencies, the *Nature Conservancy* with its prime responsibility for conservation, the *Forestry Commission*, and the *Countryside Commission*, there is now a Minister of the Environment, with overriding responsibilities for the whole of our environment, and a research unit to advise on all problems, and there is also a standing Royal Commission on Pollution.

THE NATIONAL TRUST

These Government agencies are official bodies of enormous importance for the future of our countryside. In the main, they provide opportunities for us, doing the work on our behalf. But they are backed up by a whole range of voluntary societies started by individual interested people for different purposes. The British are a nation of joiners – when they see a need, they form a society to meet that need, and they run such societies for themselves. One of the best known of these is the *National Trust*. This was started by private individuals in 1895, to preserve for ever land and buildings of beauty or historic interest. Today it owns some of the most important houses and villages in Britain, as well as 300,000 acres of our finest open country, including moorland, fens, woodland, nature reserves of its own, and more than a third of our most beautiful remaining unspoilt coastline. An example of outstanding importance for the naturalist is the Farne Islands, about 30 islands off the Northumberland coast used as a breeding place by grey seals and many sea birds – eider-duck, guillemot, puffin, fulmar, and others. In the Lake District the Trust owns more than 70,000 acres of fell and farmland, including much of the finest lake and mountain scenery. For a yearly subscription you can join the Trust, and this gives you free entry to about 200 properties, and many other privileges. Young people over 16 can join Acorn Camps, working holiday camps where you can spend a week or two giving physical help to the Trust – clearing scrub, making paths, restoring parts of buildings. Details from the Trust, at the address below.

OPPORTUNITIES FOR YOUNG PEOPLE

Quite different again, but also offering opportunities for young people, is the *Royal Society for the Protection of Birds*, founded as long ago as 1889. This is the R.S.P.B., perhaps the most famous initials of all. It really needs a whole book to itself. Again it is an entirely self-supporting organization, run on subscription, and its function is to protect wild birds, to spread knowledge and love of birds, to maintain its own bird reserves (29 of them) and to encourage interest and research. The fact that most of our wild birds are protected by law is due to the Society's propaganda. It also runs the *Young Ornithologists' Club*, for people up to the age of 18, to give them opportunities for education and field work. Write to them for information and advice on holiday courses, field outings, projects, competitions, and copies of its quarterly publication *Bird Life*, and its *Newsletter*. A very small subscription is payable. The *British Trust for Ornithology* lays special emphasis on study and work in the field, and the *Wildfowl Trust* has two remarkable collections of wildfowl, at Slimbridge in Gloucestershire and Peakirk near Peterborough.

THE COUNTY NATURALISTS' TRUSTS

Perhaps the most remarkable development of recent years in the whole history of conservation has been the growth of the various *County Naturalists' Trusts*. In many ways it is a pity they haven't a more distinctive name, because people tend to confuse them with some of the other bodies working in the same cause, and don't realize just how important and astonishing their achievements have been, and continue to be. The original energizing force behind them was a Society known as the *Society for the Promotion of Nature Reserves* (the S.P.N.R. – initials well known and revered by conservationists, because the Society has had a tremendous influence since 1912, when it was formed). As one result of its inspiration, the Norfolk Naturalists' Trust was set up in 1926, as a charitable trust to acquire nature reserves in Norfolk. It was not until 1946 that a second County Trust was formed, this time in Yorkshire, but the movement soon gained enormous impetus, so that by 1970 there were 39 trusts covering the whole of England, Wales and Scotland, with over 40,000 members managing more than 400 reserves, and this is by no means the end of the story. Each trust is a separate concern, run by committees of its own members, and raising money by private subscription.

The work of the County Trusts is far too various to be summarized. Wherever you live, you can join one of them, for a subscription, and some of them are very active indeed, with meetings, lectures, field expeditions, and opportunities for active work such as digging ditches, clearing scrub, building banks, and acting as wardens on reserves. Some of them have junior branches, mostly for people of the teenage group. Their really important work is the acquiring and management of local nature reserves. It was a local schoolboy who inspired the creation of a nature reserve at Old Slade, in the busy Colne Valley about five miles from Slough. He saw the possibilities of wet pits formed by large-scale gravel extraction. The result today is a most interesting reserve, an oasis of protected wild life in a very busy area. Over 200 plants and 100 birds have been recorded, many of them uncommon, and the reserve is used by many natural history societies for interesting work. The reserve is one of the many managed by B.B.O.N.T., odd but intriguing initials standing for the *Berkshire, Buckinghamshire and Oxfordshire Naturalists' Trust*. This is a very active Trust indeed and the record of its first ten years, published in 1970, which was European Conservation Year, is an absolutely remarkable story of ambition and achievement.

OTHER ORGANIZATIONS

The number of organizations active in the field of natural history and conservation has grown so large that in 1958 a representative body of many of them was set up as the *Council for Nature*. Four hundred and fifty societies and trusts are members, and its monthly newsletter, *Habitat*, is widely read. For our present purpose, its most important function was to organize volunteer groups of young people for conservation work on nature reserves and on 'Operation Habitat Rescue'. A report of its first ten years work is available. Individuals and groups of young people usually between the ages of 17 and 21 have been organized to undertake the most various tasks. In Kent, at Hothfield Common, a causeway 200 feet long made of railway sleepers was laid across an entomologically interesting bog; in Wales a dam was repaired, using underwater equipment, to protect a lagoon notable as a wildfowl refuge; and in many, many places rides have been cleared, ponds dug out, fences mended, derelict army equipment removed, undergrowth cut back, and nature trails constructed. The Conservation Corps is now organized by the *British Trust for Conservation Volunteers, Ltd.* All details from them.

As a service for schools and colleges, rather than for individuals, a series of field studies centres is run by the *Field Studies Council*, and a number of hostels have been specially equipped for fieldwork facilities by the *Youth Hostels Association*. Both of these are for residential courses.

For those whose interests are not quite so active, the British Tourist Authority issues annually a leaflet giving information about two hundred and thirty-two nature trails all over the country, listing them on a county basis. The idea of nature trails started in America. Basically a trail is a signposted walk specially planned to show the visitor all the features of interest in a particular reserve or other area, and many of them have explanatory leaflets giving extra information. During National Nature Week in 1963 about 50 trails were laid, but they have become so popular that their numbers are growing every year. All the bodies mentioned have helped to start them, plus a number of others, especially Shell, the large commercial organization which also produced a gazetteer of natural history in Britain. Anyone could organize a wonderful holiday, walking these trails and making a photographic record.

Finally, mention may be made of the many zoos and wild life parks springing up in the country. These vary very much. Generally but not always their interest lies in exotic species, but there are some very fine collections. Some are run by public authorities, others by private individuals, often commercially. The London Zoo has a *Young Zoologists Club*, with four thousand members in the country between 9 and 18, and similar groups may be organized by other zoos on a local basis.

Below are given the addresses of many of the organizations chiefly concerned with conservation.

USEFUL ADDRESSES

The Nature Conservancy, 19 Belgrave Square, London, S.W.1. The Biological Records Centre is at Monks Wood Experimental Station, Abbots Ripton, Huntingdon.

The Forestry Commission, 25 Savile Row, London, W.1.

The Countryside Commission, 1 Cambridge Gate, London, N.W.1.

The National Trust, 42 Queen Anne's Gate, London, S.W.1.

The Royal Society for the Protection of Birds, The Lodge, Sandy, Bedfordshire.

The British Trust for Ornithology, Beech Grove, Tring, Hertfordshire.

The Wildfowl Trust, Slimbridge, Gloucestershire.

The Society for the Promotion of Nature Reserves, The Manor House, Alford, Lincolnshire. Information about County Trusts may be obtained from this society.

The Council for Nature, Zoological Gardens, Regent's Park, London, N.W.1.

The British Trust for Conservation Volunteers Ltd, Zoological Gardens, Regent's Park, London, N.W.1.

The Field Studies Council, 9 Devereux Court, Strand, London, W.C.2.

The Youth Hostels Association, Trevelyan House, St. Albans, Hertfordshire.

The British Tourist Authority, 64 St. James's Street, London, S.W.1.

The Young Zoologists Club, The London Zoo, Regent's Park, London, N.W.1.

12

CONSERVATION KIT

A GOOD naturalist is primarily dependent on his eyes and ears, but some well-chosen equipment for observing or recording what he finds will greatly add to the value and interest of what he is doing. The simplest equipment is best to start with, then as experience is gained progress can be made with more elaborate and expensive items.

ITEMS OF EQUIPMENT

The smaller items include notebooks (best with one side of the page unlined, for drawing), pencils, a recording board made of hardboard with a bulldog clip, to hold paper in the field, large-scale maps and a compass for extended field work, and a torch fitted with a red filter if any night work is to be undertaken. Small tins, plastic boxes and bags, nets for pond work and insect sweeping, and plastic bottles, may be required by the collector, although other forms of recording are recommended by the conservationist. Paints, coloured pencils, and chalks, and perhaps plasticine for modelling, are available in great variety. A thermometer is often useful, as changes or differences in temperature often explain things seen. For looking at the detail of specimens, a hand magnifying glass will do to start with. A three-in-one set of lenses, with magnifications of different strengths, is the most compact, and a watchmaker's lens leaving the hands free is a useful gadget. All these are obtainable for a few shillings.

After this, a bigger item to think about is a camera. The simplest possible box type is adequate for a beginning, especially for landscape, trees, and plants. The cheapest Kodak 'Instamatic' 25 camera for about three pounds, or others of the same simple kind, will take excellent black and white still photographs. The 'Instamatic' range includes more elaborate models, some with built-in flash and automatic exposure accuracy. Before you consider buying anything more elaborate, you need to think out just what you hope to do with it. Bird photography has its special fascination, but also its special dangers; until you are thoroughly experienced, and understand the ways of birds, particularly on the nest, you may do a great deal of damage by concentrating too much attention on the birds – frightening sitting birds away from their eggs, disclosing the position of their nests to predators (cats are very observant) or preventing parent birds flying freely to their nests to feed their young. In the case of many wild birds wilful disturbance of them while nesting is a punishable offence. Moreover, the truly expert bird photographer needs very expensive equipment indeed, such as a 35 mm.

CONSERVATION KIT – SOME OF THE ITEMS YOU WILL FIND USEFUL

1. COLOURED PASTELS
2. COLOURED PENCILS
3. RECORDING BOARD
4. NOTEBOOK
5. PLASTICENE
6. PAINTS
7. FIELD GLASSES
8. COMPASS
9. CAMERA
10. TORCH
11. THREE-IN-ONE SET OF MAGNIFYING LENSES

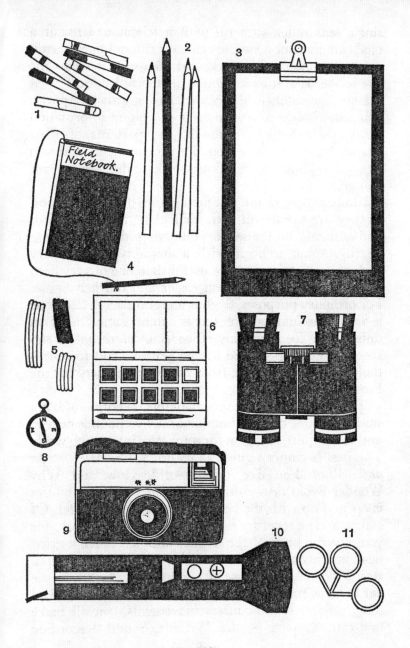

single lens reflex camera, with a telephoto lens, or a ciné camera. But a simple ordinary camera does permit some very interesting work, and the use of it trains the eye to see. If you took regular photographs at different seasons, for instance, of specimen trees in streets or parks, you would soon have a *dossier* of unique information about their habit or growth, the patterns of their branches, and their seasonable development, and you would soon find yourself noticing these things wherever you go.

Many people would put field glasses before a camera, as they are wonderful both for looking at distant birds and animals and also for observing detail in those nearby. Again, to begin with, a simple type of not very high magnification is more useful than one of very high magnification, and is much easier and quicker to use. For ordinary purposes, 8×30 is a useful size. A telescope is also a fascinating tool, but is cumbersome and often difficult to focus quickly. (See *Binoculars and Telescopes*, a guide prepared by the British Trust for Ornithology, and obtainable from the Royal Society for the Protection of Birds.)

The range of microscopes available is enormous, but a student model may be obtained for five pounds or less, and this is quite sufficient for some very interesting work. The best beginner's guide to its use is *The Microscope and What You See* (Transworld, How and Why Wonder Books). An entirely different set of possibilities is opened up with the possession of a tape recorder. Of course a tape recorder is really an expensive luxury for you, but the price of the smaller ones has fallen a great deal, and just as the use of a camera, if you can afford it, trains the eye, so the use of a sound recorder trains the ear to listen more carefully to the sounds of nature. Bird song, animal sounds, insect movements, can all make first-rate subjects – the Wildlife Sound Recording

Society once gave a prize for a recording of beetles eating dung! A lightweight portable model may be recommended, being both light to carry and easy to use. Before making one's own recordings, study of other people's is very helpful. There are a number of first-class bird song records. The best single record is perhaps *A Tapestry of Bird Song*, E.M.I. CLP1723. At the other end of the scale there is a set of twelve records from the Royal Society for the Protection of Birds, and other smaller sets produced by them. *The Sound Guide to British Birds*, from them, gives the calls and songs of 194 species on two 12″ double-sided LP records, with a 120 page book on the identification of birds by their song. Other equally interesting sets are by E.M.I., and the B.B.C.

For illustration and identification, 8 excellent bird charts are available, in two sizes, from the R.S.P.B. Another method is to build up your own collection of illustrations, either one of your own photographs or drawings, or a scrapbook using any sources available – colour supplements, magazines, or even Christmas cards. Every year beautiful Christmas cards illustrating different aspects of natural history are produced by the R.S.P.B., the various County Naturalists' Trusts, and other similar bodies. Notelets with excellent illustrations are also to be obtained, and there are some first-class postcards.

For bird gardening equipment, see *The Bird Table Book*, by Tony Soper (Pan Books), which gives a useful list of suppliers of bird food, nest boxes, and other devices for attracting birds to the garden, and recipes for bird cakes and puddings. A very wide range is obtainable from Greenrigg (Birdcraft), at Rainham, Essex, and well-made equipment is sold by the Royal Society for the Blind (Scotland). Suppliers of apparatus and stock for butterfly farming include Worldwide

Butterflies Ltd, Over Compton, near Sherborne, Dorset, and L. Christie, 137 Gleneldon Road, Streatham, London, S.W.16 (See *Create a Butterfly Garden*, by L. Hugh Newman, World's Work Ltd).

BOOKS FOR THE NATURALIST

Books for the naturalist may be numbered in thousands, at every level of knowledge, age, and expense. A beautiful series for younger children is the *Ladybird* series (Wills and Hepworth), on birds, trees, the weather, the seasons, and wild flowers. Also for very young children, the new *Storychair Book* (Transworld) includes four very attractively written, illustrated by Vera Croxford, on animals during the four seasons of the year. The *Hamlyn* all-colour paperbacks include several first-class volumes on natural history, three of these being *Bird Behaviour, Natural History Collecting*, and a *Guide to the Seashore*, all with excellent illustrations. Another first-class series of introductory books for older children are the *Clue* books, (Oxford University Press), including volumes on birds, flowers, trees and insects. These are very much more than picture books, and form by far the best introduction to the serious study of the subjects treated. The *Stand and Stare* books, published by Methuen, have an engaging small format for children, and are well illustrated; titles include insects and small animals. Six volumes in *The Private Lives of Animals* series (Warne) are much larger and more expensive, but are superbly illustrated.

Other deservedly well-known series are *The Observers' Books* (Warne) on a comprehensive list of subjects, and the *Wayside and Woodland Series* also by Warne, these being authoritative works of reference for the specialist as well as the beginner. The *Young Specialist* books published by Burke can also be recommended, particularly for the informative diagrams they contain. *Pond-Life* and *Fungi* in this series are useful.

Those of the Collins *Field and Pocket Guides* that deal with natural history in Britain and Europe are in a class by themselves. They are not only a best buy but an absolute must as soon as the reader is ready for them, being both authoritative and comprehensive. Recommended:

A Field Guide to the Butterflies of Britain and Europe
British Birds
Nest and Eggs
Wild Flowers
The Seashore
Mushrooms and Toadstools
all in this series.

Four books the enthusiast will find it hard to resist are the volumes on *Wild Flowers, Birds, Flowerless Plants*, and *Insects* published by the Oxford University Press, all well laid out and beautifully illustrated. Two other five star books are the A.A. *Book of British Birds* (Drive Publications for the Reader's Digest) and *The Concise British Flora in Colour*, by W. Keble Martin (Ebury Press).

Useful approaches to field work are suggested in some of the following books:

Adams, C. V. A. *Nature is My Hobby* (Wheaton).

Fitter, R. S. R. *Wildlife in Britain* (Penguin).

Knight, M. *The Young Field Naturalists' Guide* (Bell).

Knight, M. *Field Work for Young Naturalists* (Bell).

Leutscher, A. *Tracks and Signs of British Wild Animals* (Clever-Hulme).

Reade, W. and Stuttard, R. M. *A Handbook for Naturalists* (Evans).

Watson, G. G. *Fun with Ecology* (Kaye and Ward).

On conservation, the outstanding publication is *Nature Conservation in Britain*, by Sir Dudley Stamp (Collins). Two different aspects are dealt with in *The Vanishing Wild Life of Britain*, by B. Vesey-Fitzgerald (MacGibbon and Kee), and *Britain's Nature Reserves*, by E. M. Nicholson. Conservation on a world scale is dealt with in: *Nature's Network*, by Keith Reid, *Conservation*, by J. A. Lauwerys, and *Man's Impact on Nature*, by Joyce Joffe, all published by Aldus. A newer book to be recommended is *Conservation of Nature*, by E. Duffey (Collins International Library).

Much the best simple introduction to ecology as a general subject is *Understanding Ecology*, by Elizabeth T. Billington (Kaye and Ward, Ltd).

Most strongly recommended on the theme of the world-wide threat to wild life and to man himself are *Before Nature Dies*, by Professor Jean Dorst (Collins) and *Wild Harvest*, by Clive Roots (Lutterworth). Two great books on species in danger are *The Red Book* (Wild Life in Danger) (Collins), and *Wildlife Crisis*, by H.R.H. the Duke of Edinburgh and James Fisher (World Wildlife Fund, Hamish Hamilton).

Pollution in Britain is dealt with in *Pesticides and Pollution*, by Kenneth Mellanby (Collins), and the threat of modern tendencies to the whole of the environment is strikingly but elaborately dealt with in *Population: Resources: Environment*, by Paul and Anne Ehrlich (Freeman).

Finally, the fully-fledged advanced naturalist will find endless pleasure in the *New Naturalist Series* published by Collins. Over seventy volumes have been published, the books being roughly divided into three headings. One group deals with the background of natural history, such as *Britain's Structure and Scenery* (Sir Dudley Stamp), *British Plant Life* (W. B. Turrill), and *Climate and the British Scene* (G. Manley). The second group describes groups of animals or plants, examples being *Wild Flowers* (J. Gilmour and M. Walters), *British Mammals* (L. Harrison Matthews), and *Insect Natural History* (A. D. Imms). The third group concentrates on single areas – *Dartmoor* (L. A. Harvey and D. St. Leger-Gordon), or *The Broads* (E. A. Ellis) – or habitats such as *The Sea Shore* (C. M. Yonge) and *Mountains and Moorlands* (W. H. Pearsall). A separate series of monographs includes volumes on the badger, squirrel, rabbit, redstart, wren, greenshank, fulmar, herring gull, heron, hawfinch, house sparrow, salmon, wood-pigeon, and mole.

THE SECOND BOOK OF EXPERIMENTS
by Leonard de Vries   30p
552 54032 3   Carousel Non-Fiction

Have you ever made a thermometer or a xylophone?
This book will show you how. Some amazing scientific
experiments can be performed safely with simple every-
day things involving little cost and found in almost
every household.